An Illustrated Chronicle of the Castle and Barony of Dudley 1070 – 1757

John Hemingway

the friends of
dudley castle

An Illustrated Chronicle of
the Castle and Barony of Dudley: 1070 – 1757
John Hemingway

Published by The Friends of Dudley Castle
10 Priory Close, Dudley, West Midlands, DY1 3ED

ISBN 978-0-9553438-0-3
0-9553438-0-1

First Published July 2006
Printed by Quorum Print Services Ltd

Cover picture: Dudley Castle in the Snow
Photograph by Neil Lang

Contents

Illustrations

Cover: Dudley Castle in the Snow.

Foreword

The extent of detailed - and often most entertaining - information researched by Mr Hemingway in this remarkable volume is astounding. It is indeed wonderful that our past should be resurrected and brought to life in this way by a dedicated historian and archaeologist; who deserves our highest praise for this achievement. To illuminate the history of Dudley Castle and of its inhabitants over nearly three quarters of a millennium is to throw a broader light over the ways and customs of our people during the growth of a nation; and while some of the mores of my forbears may appear quaint today, and some even extravagant, I believe that I and my baronial cousins can on balance be proud of the part played by our ancestors in the course of that history.

Our thanks are due to Mr Hemingway for this valuable foray into Dudley's bygone days and years.

Earl of Dudley

Preface

In the mid 1980's I joined the archaeological team at Dudley Castle. My background was history, so as well as excavating I began to collect documentary references. The late Joyce Norman turned my various jottings into a story of the Barony and was ever eager for me to publish it. In 1989 the Friends of Dudley Castle were born and I serialised parts of the story in Ramparts, the Newsletter of the Friends. The problem with historians is that they are always finding new sources that open up the story. There is, however, a time when one has to stop and that time is now with the publishing of this book.

This of course is not the end, and I hope that others will follow in my footsteps and go on with the research: finding out more about the Castle and Barony of Dudley.

John Hemingway
May 2006

Barony of Dudley
Coat-of-Arms

*Figure 1: Coat of Arms of Dudley. Source: Burrell Collection
Glasgow City Council (Museums)*

1. Introduction: Ansculf of Picquigny

In the year AD 1066 Duke William of Normandy's combined Norman, French and Breton forces fought and killed the Anglo-Saxon King Harold and annihilated his English forces near a place called Hastings on the south coast. For the English this Norman Conquest was to herald great changes in their country that would affect every corner of the kingdom. Amongst Duke William's fighting men were two brothers from Picquigny on the River Somme - Ansculf and Giles. They were kinsmen, said to be younger sons of Eustace, the Videme (Lord Lieutenant) of the Bishops of Amiens, who, perhaps having few prospects of their own, decided to accompany the duke as soldiers-of-fortune [1].

Ansculf was apparently the elder man and, considering the amount of land he was subsequently given, must have fought well at the Battle of Hastings. William made Ansculf Sheriff of Buckinghamshire, and at one time Surrey [2]. He was given the lands of King Edward the Confessor, his thegn Ulf, Earl Tostig, King Harold and Archbishop Stigand [3], which would imply he was very well thought of by the King.

These lands included:

Buckingham
Newport (Paganell), Tickford, Little Woolstone, Cheddington, North Marston, Ellesborough, Stoke Poges, Ditton, Little Hampden, Lammu, Chichley, Hoggeston, Hardmead, Milton Keynes, Great Linford, Bradwell, Marsh Gibbon, Stone, Swanbourne, Soulbury, Hollingdon, Littlecote, Caldecote, Tyringham and Moulesoe.

Berkshire
Yattendon, East Isley, Hodcott, Englefield, Bradfield, Stanford Dingley, Hartridge, Compton Beauchamp, Kingston Bagpuize, Inkpen and Ufton Reading.

Surrey
Wandsworth, Milton, Abinger, Paddington, Whitford, Mitcham, Anstie & Littlefield.

Middlesex
Oxford, Cranford, Sibford, Drayton.

Figure 2: Map of Home Counties Estates. Ansculf of Picquigny was given the post of Sheriff of Buckingham after the Battle of Hastings in 1066. These were the estates that were associated with that role.

Rutland
Tolethorpe

Northampton
Barnack
Huntingdon
Waresley   [4]

The total value of these estates was a reasonable fortune amounting to £191.15.11 [5]. Ansculf had been well rewarded.

The fighting with the English was not over however. Although the brothers Edwin, Earl of Mercia (the midlands) and Morcar, Earl of Northumbria, initially made peace with the new king, it did not last. Earl Edwin, as the senior Englishmen left in the kingdom, expected to be treated accordingly, and had his eye on one of King William's daughters. Noble women were of diplomatic value, but as Edwin had nothing William wanted, a marriage was not forthcoming. With his hopes dashed, the Earl absconded to the north, where he was involved in a rebellion against the king. The Northern Rising was easily put down by William, who reacted to the instability of the north by practicing a scorched earth policy in Yorkshire, killing people and animals and burning down villages and crops. In a society where you lived on what you grew, if it was all destroyed your life expectancy would be dramatically cut short to a matter of months rather than years [6].

The king pardoned Edwin and Morcar with the proviso of no more risings, but it was not in their hands to promise anything. In East Anglia Hereward the Wake began his own war with the Normans, and in the west midlands Edric the Wild started another one. Edric, a native of Hereford/Shropshire, with support from Welsh princes, Blethgent and Rithwalan, began by attacking the Norman garrisons in Hereford in 1067, and gradually drove the Normans out of the west. King William was meanwhile in Lincolnshire waiting for the King of Denmark's sons to invade. He could not leave Edric to take over the midlands, so marched his forces across England and met Edric in battle at Stafford. The Anglo-Welsh army was defeated and then the king turned his army around and went back to the east coast. Edric was not finished however, and raised another army which occupied Chester. King William was in Yorkshire, and force marched his troops in midwinter over the snow covered Pennines and surprised Edric's forces, who were finally defeated. This time the king decided to teach the inhabitants a lesson that they would not forget, and marched through Staffordshire and Shropshire leaving a wide swathe of destruction in his wake [7].

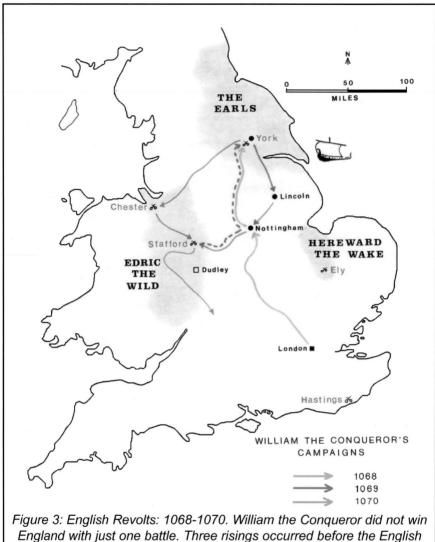

Figure 3: English Revolts: 1068-1070. William the Conqueror did not win England with just one battle. Three risings occurred before the English were subjugated.

Earl Edwin, fearing the king's wrath, tried to escape to Scotland, but was assassinated on the way. William did not trust the border lands at all, and after rampaging through their territory, he decided they needed watching very carefully. Castles were built at strategic points: Chester, Shrewsbury, Stafford and Bridgnorth as a front line. The second line of defence included Tutbury, Tamworth and Dudley. The men he put in charge of the marches were given more authority than other barons. Cheshire for instance was made into a palatinate earldom. The Earl of Chester acted as a king in his lands. This independence of the marcher lords would eventually backfire on William and his successors. Even so the king selected these men carefully.

Ansculf was obviously in the king's eye, so it is likely that he had been a senior officer in the harrying of the north and west. It is probable that William left him in the midlands after 1070 to supervise the defences of south Staffordshire. Whether it was he or the king that chose Dudley as a site for the castle is unknown, but it was well chosen. Situated on the backbone of England, with ancient routes going north to south and east to west, anyone wishing to travel east from Bridgnorth or south from Shrewsbury would have to draw near its territory. Besides which the surrounding lands had belonged to Earl Edwin, who was now dead, so it was now available.

By putting Ansculf in charge of a war zone the king was promoting him yet again. From merely being a sheriff Ansculf was now elevated to a baron; however as Baron of Dudley he needed more estates to support his position, and King William gave them to him.

Staffordshire
Aldridge, Enville, Crockington, Oxley, Sedgley, houses in Stafford, Amblecote, Upper Penn, Essington, Lower Penn, Moseley, West Bromwich, Trysull, Orton, Pendeford, Himley, Wombourne, Ettingshall, Handsworth, Cippemore, Bushbury, Rushall, Great Barr, Bradley, Perry Barr, Morfe and Chasepool.

Worcestershire
Dudley, Selly Oak, Bartley Green, Oldswinford, Frankley, Churchill, Cradley, Hagley, Bell Hall, Warley, Willingwick, Northfield, Bellington and Pedmore.

Warwickshire
Aston, Erdington, Birmingham, Edgbaston, Witton and Over.

These lands were not as valuable as those in the Home Counties, and the total value only came to £61.5.4. This is due to the fact that agriculture was the main source of wealth. The high country of the west midlands had never had rich soil to grow crops on, and consequently the population of the area was comparatively small.

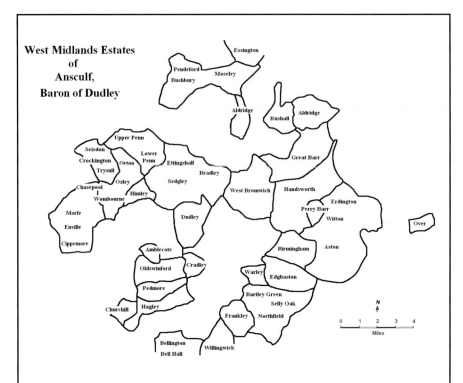

West Midlands Estates of Ansculf, Baron of Dudley

Figure 4: Map of West Midlands Estates. After the border insurrection in 1070 Ansculf was created Baron of Dudley and became the castle ward of Dudley Castle. These were the estates that were associated with that post.

2. The House of Ansculf - the First Castle

Ansculf of Picquigny: 1st Baron Dudley

The main estate in the area of Dudley was the Earl's manor of Sedgley. It was by far the most valuable of the surrounding estates, and this Ansculf held off the king. Although the ancient Ridgeway ran right through the estate, in the south east corner two hilly outcrops were completely separate from the Ridgeway. Due to the difficulty of an enemy making an assault on these hills, one of them was chosen to build his fortifications on [8]. The hill he chose was the closest one to the Ridgeway. This was the site of "Dudley" Castle - which for most of its subsequent life was included in the royal estate of Sedgley [9].

The type of fortification that Ansculf built was a reasonably quickly and cheaply erected motte and bailey that had evolved in Normandy. They even prefabricated some of them, like the one William had used at Hastings before the battle in 1066. At Dudley it was composed of a central mound surrounded by a ditch or moat on which a wooden or stone tower was erected. This was attached to a comparatively level area within a palisade, called a bailey, and was surrounded by a moat (the rock and soil from this excavation all went to build the mound or motte). The Motte is the only item that can be seen of this first castle at Dudley.

The Motte tower was the last resort in an assault and this was where the lord resided. The basement was for storage (the only access was from the first floor). The first floor was a hall or living area and the second floor a sleeping area. The third floor was a fighting platform. Nothing of this was found during the 1980's excavation, as the motte had the top removed at a later date. The Bailey was the flat area below the motte. It was used to billet and feed troops and their horses. There would have been a hall, kitchens, blacksmith and stables (there was a blacksmith mentioned in Domesday Book, but it was not stated whether he belonged to the community or to the castle).

William the Conqueror accepted the law of the land once he took over England, and one of the things this demanded from every man was that he engage in building fortifications. This might explain the Anglo-Saxon brooch found during excavations of the motte which had obviously been lost while working on the construction by an Englishman.

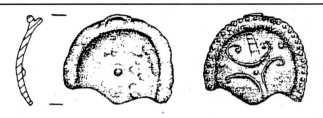

Figure 5: Anglo-Saxon brooch found during an excavation into the motte make up. The English were obliged to build fortifications if asked to do so. It was probably one of the conscripts who lost this at the time of the building of the mound.

Ansculf had become a very rich and influential man by coming to England. We have no idea where or when his life ended - whether fighting for the king or peacefully in his own bed at Dudley or Newport Paganell.

Dudley Castle, Circa 1086.

Figure 6: Reconstruction of Motte and Bailey Castle at Dudley. The Motte and Bailey was probably built by King William to control the routes out of Wales and the north west midlands. Ansculf was put in charge of it. Only the Motte still stands from this early castle.

William Fitz Ansculf: 2nd Baron Dudley

Ansculf was succeeded by his son, William, a man we even know less about! On the 1st August 1086 King William gathered all his barons to a great court held in Salisbury - presumably William Fitz Ansculf was there. The court was held in order to get the barons to swear fealty to the king, already revolts by Normans had occurred on the Welsh Marches against him. The king at the same time reorganised the services that he expected off his barons. The main service was that when asked to a baron would supply fighting men up to forty days a year; how many depended on how much land he held. William did homage for fifty two knights.

Home Counties	West Midlands
Buckingham - 6½	Staffordshire - 17½
Berkshire - 10	Warwickshire - 4½
Surrey - 3	Worcestershire - 10½
Total 19½	32½

As can be seen from the above tabulation, the west midlands supplied a disproportionate amount of knights compared to the Home Counties, this is in spite of the fact that the western estates were worth less. This is partly because the knights were situated in an area where they were thought to be needed, and partly because Dudley was the centre of the barony, but it still can be considered that the Home Counties were getting off lightly. As well as supplying knights, the knights in turn would have to provide men-at-arms. These generally numbered five per knight. The military retinue of a baron of Dudley was about 310 fighting men. This did not include mercenaries, friends and relations and other men who flocked to the banner in the hope of a war making them rich and famous.

At the same time as the Salisbury meeting, King William decided to have an inventory made of all the lands that were held in England. This was such an ambitious project that the English compared it with the list that was supposed to be made at the end of the world and called it the Domesday Book.

Domesday Book: Dudley extract

'Item William is the tenant of DUDELEI, his castle is there.
Count Edwin held the manor. It was 1 hide. In lordship 1 plough; 3 villeins, 10 borders and 1 smith with 10 ploughs, 2 slaves. Woodland: ½ league long and three furlongs wide.
Value during the reign of King Edward was £4, it is now £3.'

The information concerning Dudley shows it to have been a very small estate, but it did have a church, St Edmunds, and presumably the three farmers, ten smallholders and two slaves lived in a village at the foot of the castle with their families. The woodland was enormous, occupying nearly two thirds of the estate, and the smith is the only man of that profession recorded in the area.

We do not know what happened to William Fitz Ansculf. He may have died young and without having any children. A kinsman was recorded in a charter of one of his successors, which implies that he did not succeed because the land was taken off the family. It is possible that William joined one of the Marcher rebellions against King William II, in particular the 1095 revolt, when his successor is found to be holding the lands of another conspirator.

3. The House of Paganell

Figure 7: Arms of Paganell

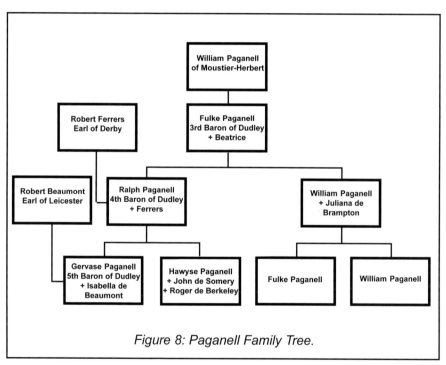

Figure 8: Paganell Family Tree.

Fulke Paganell: 3rd Baron Dudley

Fulke was not one of the original Normans to come to England. He was a younger son of William of Moustier-Herbert in France and nephew of Ralph Paganell of Drax in Yorkshire [10]. As such his inheritance was not very large, consisting of only one estate in France - Rouelle, so it is probable that he tried to improve his fortune by coming to England. It is possible that he came over in William the Conqueror's entourage in 1085, when the king is said to have brought a large force of mounted men and infantry from France and Brittany *'than had ever come before'* [11]. His father did own property in England, as he founded the Abbey of Hamble in Hampshire, and so it was not as if it was a completely foreign place to him.

How Fulke acquired the barony of Dudley is a mystery. Some historians considered that he married a daughter of William Fitz Ansculf, but there is no proof of this, nor even that William had a daughter. An alternative suggestion is that the Baron of Dudley was involved in one of the rebellions against King William II. This is based on the reasoning that Fulke is recorded as receiving the lands that had been the property of the Bishop of Coutance. The Bishop had been implicated in the 1095 rebellion, the results of which led to the perpetrators losing their lands and estates. Fulke may have received other lands of rebels - the barony of William Fitz Ansculf for instance [12].

Fulke Paganell was Baron of Dudley by 1100, and gave his name to an important seat of the Dudley Paganell's - Newport Paganel. It is also likely that he founded the Cluniac priory of Tickford close by, as it was a cell of his father's establishment at Marmoustier in France [13]. Apart from a fine paid to King Henry I of 10 marks in a plea between himself and John Parles of Handsworth in 1129-30, and evidence of him being enfeoffed of at least part of Wolverhampton, there is very little documentary evidence to go on in Fulke's time [14].

During Fulke's barony, King William II was constantly at war in France, either against his brother Robert, Duke of Normandy, or the French king. English fighting men were at their premium at the time, and it is likely that Fulke, for most of his life, was back in France fighting. It is just as likely however that he had not forgotten Dudley, and had slowly begun to convert the wooden defences of the motte and bailey construction into a stone castle.

Ralph Paganell, 1130's-1150: 4th Baron Dudley

Fulke's eldest son Ralph inherited the barony on his father's demise sometime in the early 1130's [15]. Ralph had married the daughter of a powerful local baron, Robert Ferrers, lord of Tutbury and Earl of Derby, but it is likely that Ralph was considered to be an important man in the midlands in his own right [16]. By the 1130's however, the situation in England was getting tense. Henry I had died and his nephew Stephen had been proclaimed king over the head of Henry's daughter Matilda. Matilda, upset by this slight, began a civil war with the help of her step brother, Robert, Earl of Gloucester. Most of the barons in the west supported Matilda, and Robert and Ralph were no exception.

The deteriorating situation, and the fact that Stephen lost control, meant that many of the barons began to improve their castles [17]. It seems likely that the conversion to stone of the castle at Dudley was completed at this time. The surrounding walls at least were finished by 1138, just in time for King Stephen to lay siege to it. Stephen was a professional besieger, but even he failed to make a dent in its defences. The new stone castle had been well built! In frustration the king laid waste to the surrounding territory, burning houses, and stealing cattle, before going on to see if Shrewsbury was any easier [18].

Although, according to contemporary chroniclers, Ralph subsequently made peace with King Stephen, it was not to last. Two years later he was with Earl Robert, fighting King Stephen at Lincoln. The king lost that battle and was captured with, amongst others, William Peverell, Governor of Nottingham. With apparently the war now over, Earl Robert sent Ralph to Nottingham as the new governor. It is not certain if Nottingham held out against Ralph, but he certainly treated it as an enemy town, and allowed his men to pillage the place. It was whilst this was going on that his soldiers burst into the house of a Nottingham merchant and demanded booty. The merchant told them all his worldly goods were in the cellar and then locked them in and set fire to the building. Purposely setting fire to a building in a town where the structures were both timber and close to one another was not a wise thing to do. The flames quickly spread, destroying both structures and people. Many of the citizens tried to escape the flames by going to the stone churches, but even they succumbed to the fire [19]. The massacre at Nottingham was regretted by Ralph, at least for his soul's sake. In recompense he requested on his death-bed that his son, Gervase, build a religious establishment in his name, which is how Dudley came to have a priory. We are not sure when Ralph died, possibly in the late 1140's, when the war was coming to an end [20].

Gervase Paganell, 1150-1194: 5th Baron Dudley

Ralph was dead by 1150, for in that year his son Gervase was signing charters as the new Baron of Dudley. The charter in question was the release of a retainer, a man called Essulf, to go and join the religious community at Lichfield Cathedral. It was the rule that a person's lord would have to give permission if he was to accept the authority of anyone else [21].

During the war, one of the most powerful supporters of King Stephen had been Robert de Beaumont, Earl of Leicester, nicknamed 'Bossu'. When the war came to an end in 1153 Stephen agreed that Matilda's son Duke Henry Plantagenet should succeed him. This signalled the Beaumont's and their adherents to become supporters of Duke Henry. Robert's son-in-law, Earl Simon de Senlis of Northampton, died in 1153, and a new husband was sought for his wife, the Countess Isabel. The fact that they found him in Gervase Paganell, Baron of Dudley, suggests that, like his father Ralph, Gervase was an important pawn in the national game of politics [22].

Gervase was in august company in the same year, as he was a witness to a grant by Duke Henry Plantagenet to Wolverhampton. The following year Duke Henry was at Dudley Castle as a guest, and it was there that he signed a charter relating to property of the Church of Worcester [23]. It must have been one of the last things he signed as Duke, for Stephen died in that year, and Henry was crowned the second king of England with that name. His marriage to Eleanor of Aquitaine had brought over half of France, thus making Henry one of the most powerful rulers in Europe.

Isabel, Countess of Northampton, was certainly married to Gervase by 1154, as she and her son by her former husband were both witnesses in a document of that year in which Gervase freed the debts of one of his Surrey tenants, a Walter Abinger [24]. Robert de Beaumont died in 1145 and he was succeeded by his son, also called Robert, nicknamed 'es Blanchemains' (Gervase's brother-in-law). Robert was just as powerful as his father and King Henry made him one of his two Justiciars. Gervase was very happy to be part of his affinity [25]. To emphasise his connection with the Beaumont's he quartered his own coat-of-arms, two blue lions passant on a yellow background, with the Beaumont's arms [26]. It was to Robert's favourite charity, the nuns of Kintbury, that Gervase gave his mill at Inkpen in Berkshire. The nuns moved to (Nun)eaton in the following year, 1155, but they kept Inkpen Mill [27].

Although the barons held their lands on military tenure, subsequent kings of England preferred to pick their own fighting men. Many of the second and third generation of lords thought this was quite acceptable, but the soldiers still had to be paid for. Consequently every lord was assessed at supplying 'x' number of knights, and should they by reason of age, ill health or inclination not want to fight, they would pay a knights fee in lieu of active service. King Henry II reassessed this list in 1166, and knights service as owed in 1135 were taken as the standard. Gervase was shown to be certified as supplying 50 knights, and this was what he was charged if he did not want to fight. The fact that this was a money game can be seen in the fact knights fees were divided into fractions. In 1166 for instance Gervase granted 1/5th of a knight's fee at Saltley to Henry of Rugby. Amongst the witnesses to this charter was Hawyse, Gervase's sister, and her husband Sir John de Somery [28].

Attached to a charter of land Gervase gave to Tickford Priory in 1187 is a seal showing him in what was then up-to-date military attire. He is wearing a coif - a chain mail hood with a mail veil (ventail) strapped across the lower part of his face) - a mail shirt (hauberk) with sleeves, and mail leggings. On top of this is a tunic surcoat and leggings which appear to be lower than his feet (knights are shown wearing surcoats only after 1150). He seems to be

wearing a round-topped helm with two ribbons attached, and is carrying a short shield with his coat-of-arms - the two blue lions of Dudley. This is a very early example of a heraldic reference, as these devices were still in their infancy in this period. He is shown riding his horse, which appears to be jumping into battle. Note the wicked looking spur and the stirrup [29].

Figure 9: Seal of Gervase Paganell, 1187

King Henry had inspired the institution of his friend Thomas a' Becket as Archbishop of Canterbury with the understanding he would then control both the church and state in England. Therefore his disappointment was most profound when Archbishop Thomas began to ignore his orders. This culminated in the king seeking to 'rid himself of this priest', and Thomas's subsequent murder in 1170. This action began to sour relations with many of his supporters. Gervase started to show an interest in the company of the king's eldest son, Prince Henry. He witnessed a charter of the prince's at Woodstock in the same year as the murder. The disaffection broke out three years later with the intent of putting Prince Henry on the throne. The conspirators were the King of Scotland, the Earls of Derby (Robert Ferrers - cousin to Gervase), Chester (Hugh Bigod), Norfolk (Roger de Mowbray) and Leicester (Robert de Beaumont - brother-in-law to Gervase) and Gervase himself. Fortunately for King Henry, the forces against him were disorganised and he had them all arrested. Treason is a capital offence, but he had to execute them all or none of them. As he had no intention of putting to death his eldest son, he was magnanimous in only demolishing all their castles and fining them [30]. Gervase must have made peace with Henry, as after paying a fine of 500 marks, he was *'allowed to repair in part that which he dismantled'*. His fines were paid over four years - 350 marks in 1177 and 150 marks in 1178/9 [31].

Due to the de Somery rebuild in the late 13th century it is difficult to decide on how much of the 12th century castle was destroyed when it was sleighted, and how much by Roger de Somery's new castle project. It has been popular to see a total abandonment of the site after 1175, but to judge by the above fines this is probably not the case. Whatever the defences were like, it is likely that the internal buildings could and were still lived in.

The end of the war perhaps brought out the commercial instinct in Gervase, as it did with many of his contemporaries. It perhaps started with traders coming up to the castle to sell their goods. Then country people would turn up and buy them, and thus an embryonic market came about in Dudley. There is no clue as to when this was formalised, but it was possibly in Gervase's time. The open fields on either side of the east-west road to the castle were enclosed and divided into burgage plots [32]. Judging by later evidence, most of the burgesses were local people who had traditional rights in the open fields. Presumably their burgage plot was in proportion to their earlier field holding. These rights could also be sold, allowing outsiders to become Dudley burgesses, but it is interesting how often local names continue to appear in the various documentary sources.

A new church was built in Dudley at the other end of the town to the pre-existing St Edmunds [33]. St Edmunds continued to be the parish church of Dudley, a role that continued, more or less, right up to the 17th century. On topographical grounds it looks as if the town grew from east to west, St Edmunds occupying the earliest part. The new church was built at the western end of the town on the highest point and dedicated to St Thomas a' Becket [34]. The dedication is somewhat amusing in the sense that Gervase has been considered to be getting his own back for the failed coup by dedicating it to a man King Henry II had come to detest. St Thomas was a chapel to St Edmunds, and there was never more than one vicar in the parish of Dudley [35].

Another creation that Gervase was involved in was following his father's wishes and founding a priory at Dudley. The Priory of St James was first thought about in the 1150's, when land was put aside for it. Gervase, his wife Countess Isabel of Northampton and her son Robert are recorded as making the largest endowments. This consisted of the land that the Priory was built on, plough lands in the open fields of Dudley and land across the parish bound-

Figure 10: St James Priory. The building of St James Priory was begun in the 12th century. Source: Mike Hessey.

ary in Sedgley, together with the advowson of the churches of Northfield in Worcestershire, Inkpen in Buckinghamshire and Bradfield with the chapel of Englefield in Berkshire [36].

With the initial endowment Gervase also gave the monks permission to quarry stone in order to build the church and to take timber from his woods, but it was stipulated that they were not to take any wood from the parks. The parks in question were Old Park (Wrens Nest) and Coneygre (Castle Hill). The monks were granted, *with their tenants,* the right to pasture cattle in Gervase's pasture lands and to gather pannage (acorns and mast - food for pigs) in his own woods. The term tenant may have just been legalistic formulae to cover all eventualities, but it may also imply that Gervase gave away some demesne land - land that he held personally.

The priory site Gervase gave the monks was situated in the upper part of a small north sloping valley between the high lands of Castle Hill, the town of Dudley and Wrens Nest. The northern part of the valley, in the parish of Sedgley, had been set aside as a hunting range, the aforementioned Old Park. The southern side, in Dudley, may originally have been part of it. Given the undulating land and the fact that a number of streams once flowed into it making it very wet, it could not have been prime agricultural land. The priory was confirmed in 1182, when Prior Everard oversaw Pope Lucius III's Bull of Confirmation on 16th June. The witness list included Gervase, Countess Isabel and her son Robert and Gervase's nephew Ralph de Somery (John and Hawyse's son), but by that time Gervase seemed to be losing interest in Dudley.

In Ralph's day he had put all his affairs into the hands of his steward Ralph of Barnack (from Northampton), but Gervase gave the job in the midlands to a midlander - Peter de Birmingham [37]. Peter was no servant; he held the largest unit of Paganell land in the midlands, a total of 9 knights' fees and was very capable of conducting Gervase's business. He seems to have been in regular attendance at the court of Henry II on behalf of Gervase, and witnessed royal charters there. He was succeeded by Alan, possibly his son, in 1176 [38].

In a charter of 1175 there is a reference to Gervase granting land at Brierley in Wolverhampton (actually in the parish of Sedgley) to a Beatrice of Wolverhampton. Earlier evidence of the Paganell's owning at least a part of that town is an undated document which explains how a 30½ acre freehold was owned by Fulke. Whether this was all the land they held there is not known, but if it was, it was a valuable interest, valuable enough for King John in 1205 to want it and exchange it with Kingswinford, Mere and Clent [39].

Gervase was an old man of at least 60 when he attended the coronation of King Richard The-Lion-Heart in 1189, but excused himself from accompanying the king on his Crusade to the Holy Land the following year. He paid the knights fees (called a scutage) instead and returned home to Newport Paganell. His last years seem to have been spent in giving lands to Tickford Priory. In 1187 he gave them Aston Church (Birmingham) with its dependencies of Yardley, Water Orton and Castle Bromwich. His last gift to Tickford was a house in Newport Paganell, which they received in the year of his death - 1194. He was buried in the priory church at Tickford [40].

4. The House of Somery

Figure 11: Arms of Somery family.

Ralph de Somery, 1194-1210: 6th Baron Dudley

The Somery's may have originated in Sommery in Picardy, France; presumably coming to England at the time of the Norman Conquest. A Roger de Sommery is recorded in the Domesday Book of 1086 as holding a single property in Essex, an estate called Elmdon. The fact that this was a small holding suggests the family did not have a particularly high status at that time, but at present it is not possible to tie this family with the Dudley Somery's [41].

The Dudley family appears about a hundred years later, when Sir John de Somery married Hawyse Paganell (Gervase's sister). It seems to have been the custom with the barony of Dudley that if there was no heir to the baron then the barony reverted to a brother or a sister. Sir John had probably died before 1182 and Hawyse's second husband was Roger de Berkeley [42]. She still inherited the dower lands of the Barony of Dudley and Ralph paid a fine of £100 and two palfreys to get these back on her death in 1208 [43].

According to a Pipe Roll, Ralph paid to be accepted as Baron of Dudley a fee of £43.19s.2d in 1194. Grazebrook observed that Ralph travelled to Germany while King Richard was still in prison to be invested in his uncle's title. In fact Ralph paid 33 marks for Gervase's lands [44]. Quite what Ralph had inherited is open to question as his mother seems to have held on to Newport, at least until her death. The fact that Ralph was involved in an inquisition into the advowson of the Church of Bradfield in Berkshire held by Dudley Priory, may suggest he was looking around for any income available.

Ralph probably spent a lot of his time in military pursuits. In the Curia Regis Rolls, Ralph is shown *'beyond the sea'* in 1199, presumably fighting the French with King Richard. Richard died in the April of that year. A document of 1203 vouched that the *'Barons Perceval de Somery held 50 knights*

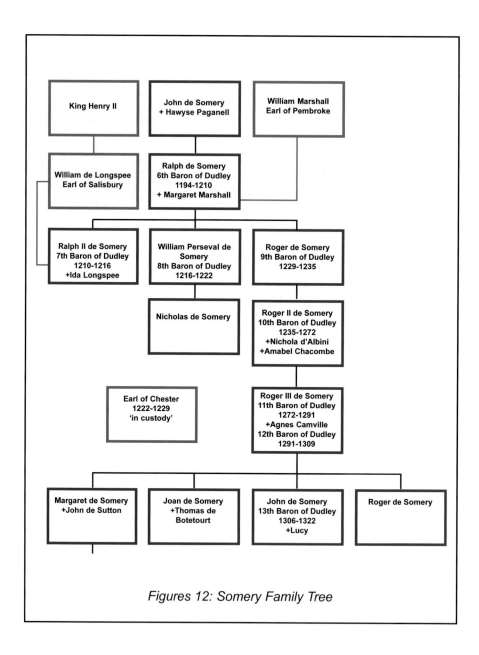

Figures 12: Somery Family Tree

King Henry II

John de Somery
+ Hawyse Paganell

William Marshall
Earl of Pembroke

William de Longspee
Earl of Salisbury

Ralph de Somery
6th Baron of Dudley
1194-1210
+ Margaret Marshall

Ralph II de Somery
7th Baron of Dudley
1210-1216
+Ida Longspee

William Perseval de
Somery
8th Baron of Dudley
1216-1222

Roger de Somery
9th Baron of Dudley
1229-1235

Nicholas de Somery

Roger II de Somery
10th Baron of Dudley
1235-1272
+Nichola d'Albini
+Amabel Chacombe

Earl of Chester
1222-1229
'in custody'

Roger III de Somery
11th Baron of Dudley
1272-1291
+Agnes Camville
12th Baron of Dudley
1291-1309

Margaret de Somery
+John de Sutton

Joan de Somery
+Thomas de
Botetourt

John de Somery
13th Baron of Dudley
1306-1322
+Lucy

Roger de Somery

30

fees'. That there was a family connection between the Somerys and the Percivals is an interesting piece of evidence, though as of yet we can make very little of it. King John inherited a bad situation which he did not improve, and the fighting in France came to an end when Normandy fell to the French in 1204. With the fall of France came the loss of Rouelle in Normandy, the only French Paganell-Somery property.

As King Richard had virtually bankrupted the country during the crusades, his brother King John badly needed ready cash to pay his fighting men. One way in which he could gain this money was to own market centres. This was the reasoning in 1205 behind a suggestion to Ralph that he may like to swap Wolverhampton for the royal estates of (Kings) Swinford, Clent and Mere. The king did not like refusals so Ralph gave him Wolverhampton [45]. Like the later Gervase he rarely had much to do with his midland estates, although there is a charter of 1208 where he attests between Walter Bagot and Thomas de Erdington, but little else [46].

Ralph retrieved the barony of Dudley's lands on his mother's death in 1208, but only survived her by a year. Like his uncle, Ralph was very generous to Tickford Priory, giving them land and property. Ralph's wife was called Margaret and she was the sister of William Marshall, Earl of Pembroke. William Marshall became her guarantor in a legal action to claim her dower on Ralph's death in 1210 [47]. On the death of Ralph she remarried. Maurice de Gant of Berkeley. Maurice's son Roger held some Dudley lands in the time of Roger de Somery I [48].

Ralph de Somery, 1210-1216: 7th Baron Dudley

Ralph II is an obscure person; many historians did not recognise that he existed as he did not survive his father by many years, but he seems to have been the eldest son of Ralph I. In the Book of Fees 1212-1215 he is shown to be the ward of William Longspee, Earl of Salisbury (an illegitimate son of Henry II), but only 10½ fees of the barony's 50 were held by him, which suggests his mother, Margaret, held the rest. As it was normal for a ward to be with his guardian, Ralph was probably at the Battle of Poitou [49]. Ralph may have come of age (21) in 1214, when the Earl of Salisbury's wardship ceased. His connection with the family did not however as Ralph married Ida Longspee, William's daughter. He was assessed of the whole barony in 1215, so presumably his mother was dead by then [50]. Nothing else is known about him other than that he was certainly dead by 1216. As he died comparatively young, perhaps he fell in battle fighting Prince Louise of France who occupied most of southern England at the time.

Ida was a typical Plantagenet, a fiery woman who brooked no opposition. Mathew Paris, a contemporary author, wrote in shocked tones of her attempt to keep the Dudley dower lands: *'Claiming to take her dower at her choice she raided the manor of Crawley, Bucks. and pulled down houses, cut down trees and did enormous damage.'* [51].

She remarried William de Beauchamp, Baron of Bedford, and they kept Newport Paganell and other home county lands of the Barony of Dudley until her death in 1268 [52].

William Percival de Somery, 1216-1222: 8th Baron Dudley

William was a younger brother of Ralph II, and he was still in his minority in 1216 when he was placed in wardship with Ranulf, Earl of Chester [53]. As William was acquitted from paying scutage in 1220 he had reached maturity, but it does suggest he was with the king's army. This was during the period of the young King Henry III's minority, when Bishop Peter de Roches of Winchester and Hubert de Burgh, the king's Justiciars, were involved in a power struggle. William was with the king's army at Witham in 1221, as he paid scutage to return home [54]. Where home was we are not quite sure, but it is interesting that documents start to appear referring to his midland estates. In 1221 he sued for a knight's fee in Ettingshall, and on April 17th 1222 he was involved in a fine for 16 acres of Bradley, Bilston. He also leased out a tenement to Ranulf Langde in Oldswinford for 3 shillings and 6 pence in the same year, after which nothing is heard of him [55].

Nicholas de Somery, 1222-1229

William's son Nicholas was only a child when his father died and his lands were held in wardship, like his father's had been, by the Earl of Chester. In 1226 Nicholas as heir to *'Percival de Somery'* was said to hold *Bordesleigh* (Bordesley) *'in the custody of Chester'* [56]. This was a new property of the Dudley's, and it vanished as quickly as it appeared. Nicholas is mentioned again in 1228 and apparently died in Worcestershire (Dudley) in the summer of 1229, still in his minority. A Fine Roll of 4th July 1229 commissioned the Sheriff of Worcester to seize all the lands of the late Nicholas de Somery, save those of the king and Earl of Chester [57].

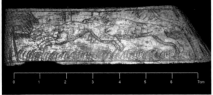

Above: The bone plaques were probably two sides of a knife handle and show a hunting scene - hounds hunting a boar.

Below: The bone plaque shows a series of buildings with a large gateway in the centre. Whether this is supposed to be Dudley Castle or any other place is unknown.

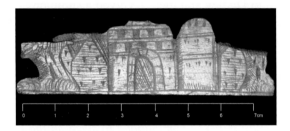

Figure 13: Inscribed bone found at Dudley Castle in the 1980's archaeological excavations. Source: Dr Richard Thomas.

Roger de Somery I, 1229-1235: 9th Baron Dudley

Roger was a younger brother of Ralph II and William Percival and, as a younger son, he would not have considered it likely that he would have inherited the barony; therefore he had made a military career for himself. His lack of interest resulted in him conveying his estates of Dudley, Sedgley, Mere, Clent and Swinford, plus advowsons and churches to Roger de Gaunt (of Berkeley) for 7 years from Michaelmas 13 Henry III (1221) and stated that he was not to have married within that term [58]. This is an odd document as it appears to be saying it is a 1229 copy of a 1221 charter! Roger de Gaunt is likely to have been Roger's step brother, and perhaps had an interest in the property from their mother. As it is a conveyance from Roger it also appears to suggest Roger has leased Dudley etc from his brother William or his nephew Nicholas and then re-leased it to Roger de Gaunt. This would fit as William de Beauchamp still held Newport Paganell with his wife Ida Longspee. It seems Roger received his land back by 1229.

Roger did homage for the Barony of Dudley on 10th July 1229, but was away fighting in France in the following year, as he had letters of protection signed in Portsmouth [59]. Henry III invaded France in this year to retrieve his father's (King John's) possessions. He set his court up in Nantes, but nothing came of it as the French crown grew stronger. The problem with Henry was foreign influences which upset English barons. In 1232 he invited Peter de Roches back to replace Hubert de Burgh as his adviser. In fact de Burgh was stripped of his offices and sent for trial. This particularly upset Roger's cousin, Richard Marshall, Earl of Pembroke, who started a revolt on the Welsh Marches. Roger was commanded to hold Shrewsbury against the rebels. It is difficult to determine what he felt about this idea, but either his forces were too weak or his sympathy lay with his cousin because Shrewsbury was captured and burnt [60].

Roger retired to Dudley and there received a summons from the king to attend his majesty for the purpose of receiving a knighthood. Roger did not go and it is difficult to see why unless he felt King Henry III had good reason to harm him. The result was that the king ordered the Sheriffs of Worcester and Stafford to seize all his possessions:

> *"Because Roger de Somery, at the feast of Pentecost last past, has not appeared before the king to be girded with the military girdle, the Sheriff of Worcester shire is herby commanded to seize on the house of Dudley and all other lands of the said Roger within his jurisdiction, for the king's use; and to keep them with all the cattle found upon them; so that nothing may be moved off without the king's permission."*
>
> *Witness, the King at Wenlock etc* [61].

Richard Marshall's demand for the expulsion of all *'the strangers from the royal council'* might have succeeded if he had not been killed in 1234. Ironically his widow, Henry III's sister, married again this time to a man called Simon de Montfort! Whether Roger went the same way as his cousin is not known, but he died in the following year - 1235 [62].

Figure 14: Medieval arrowheads found during excavation. Source: DUCAP.

Roger de Somery II, 1235-1272: 10th Baron Dudley

Roger's Home Counties lands were still held by his aunt, Ida de Longspee, and her husband, the Earl of Bedford, so he had to make do with what he actually held. But what he held was no mean estate. When at home he lived at his manor house at Kingswinford, but his first wife, Nicola Albini, brought Chipping Campden as part of her dowery, and he also spent time there, obtaining a market and a fair for the town in 1247. He also set up a fair at Clent in 1253 [63].

His hunting lands took special place in his life; a free warren (Coneygre, Castle Hill) was granted to him in 1247. He acquired deer to stock his 'New' Park (on the Dudley, Sedgley, Kingswinford parish bounds) and William Burdet was given hunting rights in it [64]. He took poaching seriously, as can be seen in various writs; Roger sued Richard of Wolverhampton on June 23rd 1258, and Roger de Peteshall and William de Leominster in October 1259 [65]. A dispute arose over what services were due to Roger from his steward, William de Birmingham. By this time the term steward did not necessarily mean someone who served meals, and as far as the de Birmingham's were concerned, they were important sub-lords in their own right. Therefore they thought of it as an honorary title. The case went on from 1249 to 1260, and the court's decision was that technically Roger was in the right to expect William to appear before him at monthly intervals, but in the end they agreed in future that it need only be at 6 monthly intervals [66].

Roger's second wife was Amabel de Chacombe, and she was the mother of his son and heir, also called Roger [67]. Roger II's time was not all taken up with homely sports and activities; in 1248 King Henry gave Simon de Montfort a commission to administer Gascony. By 1253, due to good government, he had managed to upset them sufficiently to start a rebellion. Roger was part of the force sent to put the insurrection down [68]. King Henry put Simon on trial in Westminster Hall and he was correctly vindicated, but the king had made a life-long enemy of his former favourite. King Henry's son was made nominally Lord of Gascony in Simon's place in 1254 and Roger paid an 'aid' for the knighting [69].

Trouble was starting closer to home in the following year when Llewellyn ap Gruffydd proclaimed himself Prince of North Wales in 1255 and proceeded to encompass the English controlled south. It got so out of hand that Roger was sent to Glamorgan to join the royal army muster, but in June the English forces were disastrously defeated near Carmarthen. The following year Llewellyn convened all the Welsh leaders and got a general agreement that he be called Prince of Wales. Roger was sent to Chester in 1258 and Hereford in

1262 to fight Llewellyn's forces, but neither campaign could oust the power of the Welsh prince [70].

The Welsh seemed to be getting dangerously close to Dudley, and it was probably this fact that prompted Roger to begin refortifying Dudley Castle in 1262. To fortify a castle needed a licence from the king, which he did not have. According to Blanow, the objection came from his fellow barons, who were wary about a royalist castle that may have been used against them rather than the king, but whatever the Sheriff of Worcester was sent to stop the work [71]. Within months Roger was ordered to muster with his forces in Hereford to commence another campaign against the Welsh.

He received a licence to fortify his castle in the following year, but by then the king had something more than Llewellyn to worry about - the start of the Baronial War [72]. This was led by the king's old favourite Simon de Montfort. The disaffection of a great number of his barons had been boiling up for some years, chiefly because of Henry's adulteration of many of the tenets of the Magna Carta signed by his father. A Parliament was held in Oxford on June 11th 1258 to sort out the differences. Roger was one of the 24 appointed on the Finance Committee, but basically all they were doing was choosing which side they were going to be on [73].

It all came to a head on the 16th March 1264, when Simon led the barons in a rebellion against the king. In May the two opposing forces met at Lewes. Roger supported the king and fought in the King of the Roman's Division with his cousin John Fitzalan, baron of Clun. They surrendered with Percy and de Bohun and were captured by Simon's forces who won the day [74]. Roger was still with the captured king in the following year when Prince Edward trapped Simon's forces at Evesham and won a resounding victory [75].

Although Simon died in the battle, the king had learned his lesson about the barons' feelings over the Great Charter, and tended to leave it well alone. The peace treaty in August 1266 at the end of the Baronial War was called the "Dictum of Kenilworth", and was designed to appeal to the survivors on both sides. Seven lords and four prelates were chosen to formulate the "Dictum", and it shows the important standing of Roger de Somery that he was selected as one of the lords.

On the death of his Aunt Ida in 1268, some of his lands in the Home Counties were returned to him, and one of Roger's last recorded acts was to grant the right to hold a market and eight day fair at Newport Paganell, and a Saturday market in Dudley [76]. Roger died sometime before August in 1272. He had spent most of his life in the midlands, and it was at his Priory at Dudley he wished to be buried. According to his Inquisition Post Mortem his castle was *"newley commenced"* but unfinished, his market in Dudley was making a profit and he had a private park in Pensnett Wood (the New Park) [77]. Another document records that poachers were caught in his park at Weoley Castle on the day of his death [78].

Roger de Somery III, 1272-1291: 11th Baron Dudley

Roger was 18 when his father died. The king's escheator seems to have taken custody of Roger's estates during his minority. On 29th August 1273, the Keeper of Roger's Parks and Chases was ordered to kill, salt and barrel venison from Dudley and Weoley, presumably for the king's use [79]. King Edward was still playing free with Roger's inheritance, as in October 1275 he ordered 24 live bucks and does (8 does and 4 bucks from the Park and 8 does and 4 bucks from the Wood) to go to Roger Mortimer to stock his park [80]. He also ordered underwood and deadwood to be sold from Roger's woods [81]. This seems to be the last bite out of the cherry, because Roger came of age in 1275 and took control over his lands. His mother died three years later

Figure 15: Keep on Motte. The de Somery keep was an old fashioned structure when it was first built. It is likely that it was a symbol that the lord wished all to see of the power of the lordship.

and before Roger received the dower lands she held, Bogo de Knovill was requested to render accounts on the ferm of the manors in fee [82].

In 1282 David, Prince Llewellyn ap Gruffydd's brother, led an uprising against the English throne, laying siege to the castles of Hawarden and Flint [83]. One by one other Marcher castles fell to the Welsh forces. Roger received a writ on the 25th March 1282 to muster at Rhuddlan with all his retainers to fight the Welsh. In fact King Edward would have preferred his money than his attendance to pay for mercenaries, but Roger was a soldier by profession. According to a Coram Rege Roll a suite between Roger and William de Bermingham was postponed till Roger came back from Wales where he was *on the kings business*. David broke into Hawarden and massacred the inhabitants, but then began to retreat into Snowdonia as King Edward's forces followed along the coast. On November 5th part of the royal army was ambushed in the mountains and the king had to redraw to Rhuddlan. On December 11th Llewellyn was killed on a foolhardy raid on Builth, but David held on till he was captured and executed in July 1283 [84].

By the Statute of Wales in 1284, the whole country became subject directly to the crown and all was peaceful - for a while! But in 1287 King Edward was away in Gascony and Rhys ap Maredudd broke into open revolt. Roger was summoned to join the Earl of Cornwall (Edward's regent) at Gloucester on the 15th July. The campaign resulted in a siege of Rhys's fairly impregnable castle of Dryslyn. A massive siege engine that needed 40-60 oxen to pull it was brought up and bombarded the walls with immense stones. Rhys was forced to surrender.

Like his father, Roger preferred the comfort of his manor houses to the castle. He resided in either Sedgley or Kingswinford when at Dudley, but Weoley was also a favourite home. Like his father he also appreciated hunting, though it did get him into trouble in 1282. It appears that he was hunting in his chase at Baggeridge when his dogs chased a stag. The animal ran for cover across what is now the A491 into the Royal Forest of Kinver. Roger sent Thomas of Wombourne and Hugh de Sapey after it. The dogs cornered it and Thomas shot it dead with his bow and arrow, killing it in the forest. They then took the venison to the manor house at Kingswinford, but they had been seen by a royal forester who confronted the two men. They explained the situation and pointed out that Roger was now at his other home at Sedgley. Although the animal may have been Roger's, once within the confines of the royal forest it was the king's. Roger was summoned to appear in parliament on what was a capital offence and fined 200 marks for his transgression [85].

Roger died in 1291 and was buried in Dudley Priory. Bishop Roger of Coventry granted an indulgence of forty days to all who should say a pater noster and an ave for the repose of his soul. This was confirmed by Pope Boniface VIII [86]. In his Inquisition Post Mortem the castle is described as the *'chief edifice of the barony'* and the value of Dudley market had increased since his father's time. His wife Agnes followed him in the barony.

Figure 16: Great Chamber Complex. Built in the time of the de Somery's, the Great Chamber was the private quarters of the Barons of Dudley. The large windows were installed by William Sharrington in the 16th century to bring the structure in line with the Renaissance range.

Agnes De Somery, 1291-1309: 12th Baron Dudley

The wardship of her eldest son John was shared between his mother Agnes and John St John, and like dowager baronesses of Dudley before, she held the honour. A Patent Roll of 1st January 1292 stated that Agnes instructed William *'de Kytremynstre'* (Kidderminster) to act as her attorney to receive her dower of knight's fees [87]. She held Bordesley, Bradfield, Weoley, Rowley and Handsworth. Her two sons John and Roger were in their early teens when their father died. John as the eldest probably lived with St John, as was the custom, while Roger stayed at home with his mother.

John St John was made Seneschal of Gascony by King Edward in 1287. The French invaded the province in 1296 and St John fought hard against the odds to defend the country. It is probable that the 15 year old John de Somery served with him as a squire. When St John was captured by the French the following year it was the custom for the squire to follow his lord into captivity, whether or not he had been captured himself [88]. A truce was signed in the October of 1297, and presumably the Seneschal and his colleagues were freed. It is likely that being 'blooded' in Gascony, John joined the king's forces in England to fight the Scots. He may have joined the 1301 campaign, and most certainly was on active service in 1302 [89].

Due to the fact that John was in wardship, the king took a cut out of the profits of his woods and chases. On 25th October 1291 the king gave Bogo de Knovill, Sheriff of Shropshire and Staffordshire, 30 live bucks from Agnes' parks in Dudley and Sedgley. Two sub-escheators were put in charge of Agnes' woods: Adam de Elmrugge and Malcolm. Malcolm settled himself nicely in Dudley Castle and to judge by the nine deer he had delivered there, dined on venison. William de Beresford, Agnes' forester, reported all transactions to the king's men. The sale of charcoal in Pensnett, Baggeridge, Old Park and Handsworth for instance was used to pay the castle servants and the foresters. Adam also 'spent' 40 deer, though he complained that Sir William Stafford of Amblecote poached 60 deer from both the New Park and his part of Pensnett Chase. The resident forester of Pensnett Chase was reported to be Henry de Imeneye and the parker of New Park John de Orsete [90].

Agnes successfully ran the barony, although there were one or two upsets. She was in debt to William de Hamelton, Archdeacon of York, in 1293, and the king held some of her lands in Rowley after she hung one of her tenants for a felony in July 1297. As she was invited to the coronation of Edward II in February 1308, all had been forgiven. In an Inquisition of Forest Holdings in 1306, she and Roger were given royal permission to have hunting rights in Prestwood and the Haye of Ashwood in the Royal Forest of *Kynfar.* As the Chetwyn family traditionally held these rights, it is possible it was part of a marriage settlement between Roger and a Chetwyn heiress [91].

Roger's predilection for hunting led to his death. In the same year as he was hunting in the Wolverhampton Woods he was allegedly murdered by Walter de Wynterton. Walter's chattels were subsequently confiscated as he 'flew' from the scene, thus making him an outlaw. The place where the 'crime' was committed was in the woods, and the fact that Walter was subsequently pardoned for it suggests it was a hunting accident, something that was far from uncommon in the period. Walter appeared before the king's justices with his pardon by which his outlawry was suspended [92].

Figure 17: Triple Gateway. The original gateway was added to in the late 13th century. It had porticoes built with portcullis and doors and a vaulted ceiling with a murder hole added.

Agnes was summoned to King Edward II's coronation in February 1308 and she died in the November of 1309. In her will she wished to be buried next to her husband in Dudley Priory and as a sweetener to the monks she gave them her part of the parish of Churchill. As she was holding the barony there was an Inquisition Post Mortem on her effects [93].

John de Somery, 1309-1322: 13th Baron Dudley

John was born at Weoley Castle on the 2nd March 1280 [94]. He came of age in 1302, but St John had sold Agnes the custody of him in 1299, so presumably he was a free agent from then up until his mother's death [95]. In 1305 war came to an end in Scotland, William Wallace was put to death and John came home to Dudley. Virtually immediately he had a row with the sub-bailiff, John Jolyf, as he charged him with breaking into one of the parks and stealing cattle in 1306 [96]. John did not stay at Dudley very long as war started again in Scotland with the crowning of Robert the Bruce as king. John by now was associated with Edward, Prince of Wales, and they were knighted together before the army moved up into Scotland. At the knighting ceremony John was dressed from the royal wardrobe [97]. The muster was at Carlisle, and from there the army marched on to Methien. A battle was fought on the 20th June, but this was the last English victory. King Edward I was by now ill and he died in the July of 1307.

John was back in Scotland in 1310, but he was only there to participate in the harrying exercises. A document of Complaint referring to poachers taking

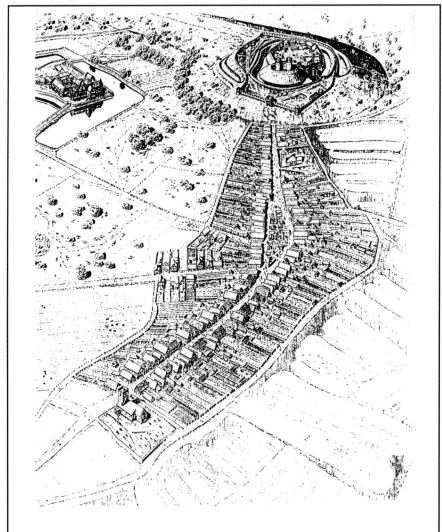

Figure 18: Reconstruction of what Dudley and its castle may have looked like in 1300. Source. DMBC Ludlow/Boland.

deer from John's parks in Dudley and Sedgley dated January 1314 stated that he was *'beyond the seas in the king's service'*. This was followed by a royal order to tax collectors in Staffordshire on 21st March 1314, to pay John £100. This is likely to mean that John was fighting for pay and that he did not necessarily have his barony knights in tow. So far we have no evidence that John was at the defeat of Bannockburn on the 22nd June, but he was called by the king, who was then at Berwick, on the 30th June to assemble at Newcastle on the 15th August for the defence of the north of England [98].

King Robert the Bruce was, however, a much more tenacious opponent than his predecessors, and slowly began to push English control further and further south until 1319. The last Scottish town to remain in English hands fell in that year. Edward's lords, who were in the process of entering a power struggle of their own, combined to besiege Berwick. John and his brother-in-law John de Sutton both had letters of protection to join the siege. They seem to have been up there for at least two years. When the Scottish lords of Moray and Douglas invaded Yorkshire, the siege of Berwick was abandoned to protect northern England. The Scottish war was over and a civil war was beginning!

King Edward II was a different type of king to his father and did not inspire either fear or love from his subjects. But what brought about his eventual fall was his bi-sexuality, with a predilection to have favourites. This would have been fine if the men in question had kept a low profile, but in the case of Piers Gaveston, a French knight, he flaunted his position and the great gifts the king gave him. In Edward's eyes he could do no wrong, and was amused the way his favourite insulted the great barons. The most powerful lord was Edward's cousin Thomas, Earl of Lancaster, who rallied around him an anti-Gaveston faction. This ill-feeling smouldered for many years.

Eventually the lords rebelled against Edward and Gaveston, and the latter was arrested at Scarborough Castle. He was brought down south, but was taken by Guy de Beauchamp, Earl of Warwick. Piers Gaveston had called him the *'Black dog of Arden'*. Guy, when he heard of this nickname, said then he would bite Piers at the first opportunity. The opportunity was now at hand, and he had him beheaded outside Warwick in 1309. John de Somery had never supported the rebel lords, and he was appointed a commissioner regarding Gaveston's lands; he also held the wardship of Guy's son of Sutton Coldfield and Studley [99]. He was given another wardship in May of 1311, that of Urien St Peter [100].

John was not always in the royal good books however, as in December 1310 he gave some plough lands to St Thomas's Hospital in Birmingham without a licence, and was reprimanded for it [101]. In important things John was faithful to the king, as was Roger Mortimer of Herefordshire and John Charlton of Powys [102]. The majority of the Staffordshire lords however were dominated by the Earl of Lancaster. One group that "ruled" the area between Cannock and Dudley was the Swynnertons. The habit of John gathering local taxes on the king's behalf generated its own ill feeling, and he was reported in 1311 to the Sheriff of Stafford:

> "... he had taken upon himself so great an authority in Staffordshire that no man could have law or reason by means thereof and that he domineered there more than a king; as also that it was no abiding for any man in these parts except he well bribed the said John de Somery for protection, or yield him much assistance towards the building of his castle and that the said John did use to beset men's houses in that country to murther them, as also extorted large sums of money from them.
> William de Bereford" [103].

This has led to nearly every historian who has ever seen this document as taking it at its face value and labelling John as some kind of thug. In fact it is part of a much larger issue. The courts at Stafford in that particular year were notorious as the Swynnertons turned up armed to the teeth and proceeded to intimidate the royal justices. The king appointed William de Tressell and Alan la Zouche to look into the allegations against John. We do not know of the results, but its possible the charge was quashed.

Although John de Swynnerton journeyed to France to attend the king at the coronation of the King of Navarre in 1314 with Charlton, Sutton (John's brother-in-law) and Somery, there was little love lost between them. When they came back to England the Swynnertons laid wait for and murdered John de Somery's tax collector, Robert de Essington. John de Swynnerton spent a year in the Marshalsea prison for this crime. John de Somery realised he needed these men if he was going to raise the standard of the king in the west midlands and he dropped the charges. The Swynnerton family agreed to recognise his power and joined his affinity. The situation grew worse however, and in the years 1318/19 attacks and reprisals between the families were common. John de Somery and his cousin Ralph Bassett were given a commission of oyer and terminer to enforce the king's peace in the area, but to no avail [104].

It would appear that John also had trouble with his own family. In 1321 Nicholas de Somery, his cousin, allegedly broke into Dudley Castle and stole goods to the value of £200 and £1000 in cash. A Richard de Tutbury and Nicholas Emold were arrested in Kent as his accomplices [105]. It was on

April 10th of that year that the King rewarded John for his faithfulness with life custody of the Manor and Forest of *Kynfar* [106].

In 1322 Edward began a campaign to reduce Lancaster's supporters, particularly on the Welsh Marches. An order dated the 15th February 1322 to John from the king to find 2,000 men-at-arms and footmen to bring into the king's service, but excused John from picking his own tenants [107].

John and Ralph Bassett were commissioned to seize Lancaster's castle of Kenilworth for the king on the 12th March [108]. John died on St Thomas's Day (July) in the same year. In his Inquisition Post Mortem the Castle chapel is mentioned for the first time. His wife Lucy held her dower of Rowley and Prestwood, but as John and Lucy never had any surviving children, his estates were divided between his sisters, Margaret, who had married John de Sutton, and Agnes, who had married John de Botetourt.

It seems there was some problem over Lucy's not getting all her dowery, as a letter written by Bishop Thomas Cobham of Worcester in the following year demanded his staff to find the perpetrators of this affair.

"It has been intimated to us on the part of William de Bourgh, executor of the last will of the noble loard j. de Someri, lately deceased and of d, John de Bromsgrave, proctor of the lady Lucy, the widow and executrix, tht certain sons of iniquity are retaining and concealing some property of the deceased, to the perial of their souls. We therefore cammand you, when so requested by the said William and John, to warn such persons under pain of greater excommunication to surrender those goods, and you are to send their names.
Hartelebury, 10th March 1323"
[109]

Figure 19: Castle Chapel. The Chapel was probably being finished off in the time of John de Somery and the early years of the Sutton's.

5. The House of Sutton

Figure 20: Arms of Sutton family.

John de Sutton I, 1322-1325: 14th Baron Dudley

John de Sutton was the descendant of a family who owned Worksop in Nottinghamshire. John's father Richard had married very well, Isabella Patrick, the sole heiress of William Patrick, Lord of Malpas Castle in Cheshire [110]. John eventually inherited both these estates. In 1307 Sir Richard Sutton (John's father) gave John and his new wife Margaret de Somery his lands at Worksop. On the surface it appears he was a very generous gentleman, but in fact he was living well above his means and he was in debt to Margaret's mother, Agnes, to the tune of £35,000. His lands were in default of payment and an agreement had been made whereby five of Sutton's manors would revert to the Somery's on Sir Richards's death if he had not repaid the debt [111]. The connection between de Suttons debt and his grandson's marriage to a de Somery, is very obvious, particularly when later Sutton marriages are taken into account. John de Sutton enfeoffed (gave) his estates to John de Somery in 1319. Whether this was in case he was killed in battle or another case of the Sutton's being in debt is not known [112].

Margaret was the elder sister of John de Somery, so consequently on his death she claimed, as was her right, the Caput or head of the Barony, but her sister Joan and her husband John de Botetourt also got a share of the estate. This was an event that often occurred in the Barony of Dudley when the Lord died, though in this case it would have financial repercussions throughout the period of the Sutton's lordship. Although John's wife Lucy was given her dower lands, she died in 1325, and they were shared out between the two sisters. On 26th November 1322, the King's Escheator was ordered to deliver Dudley Castle and associated manors to John and Margaret and John and Joan. They appeared satisfied with the division but that was not to last. They were still sorting things out in Chancery as late as 1342.

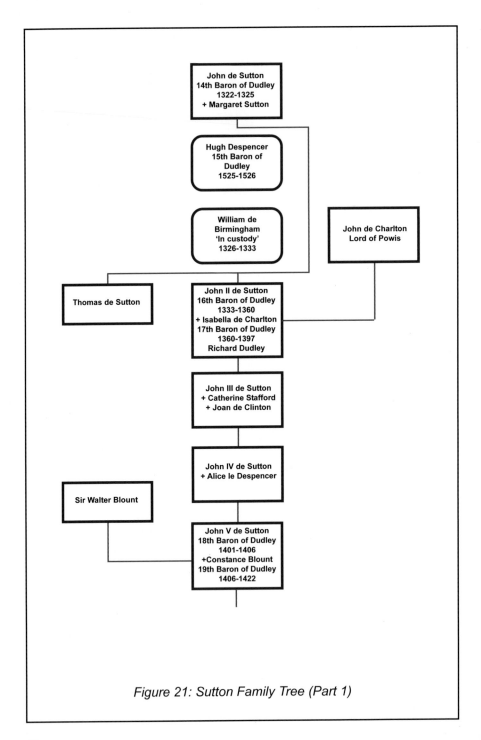

Figure 21: Sutton Family Tree (Part 1)

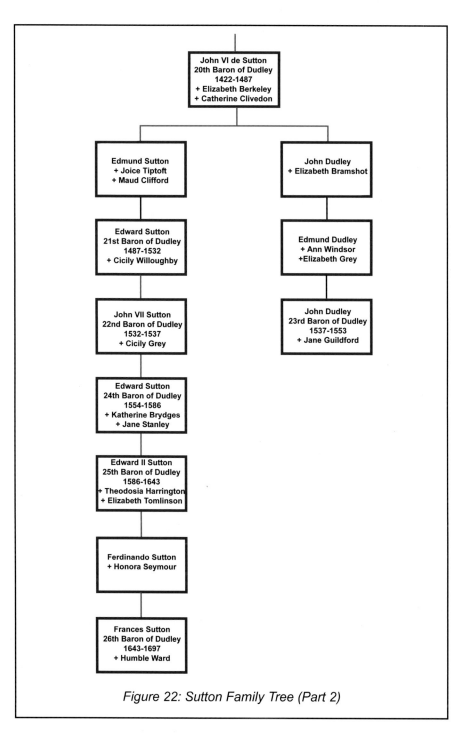

Figure 22: Sutton Family Tree (Part 2)

The Division of the Barony in 1322

| John de Sutton/ Margaret de Somery
(Barony of Dudley) | | Thomas de Botetourt/Joan de Somery | |

Worcestershire	Warwickshire	Worcestershire	Warwickshire
Dudley	Birmingham	Selly Oak	Aston
Cradley	Erdington	Bartley Green	West Bromwich
Bordesley	Edgbaston	Oldswinford Church	Castle Bromwich
Lutley	Handsworth Church	Frankley	
Willingswick	Nechells	Churchill	
Witton	Saltley	Hagley	
Dodyston	Bromwich	Bell Hall/Bellington	
		Warley	
		Northfield	
		Pedmore	

Staffordshire	Shropshire	Buckingham	Northampton
Kingswinford	Foxhale	Stoke Poges	Barnack
Evernesfield		Hoggestone	
Morfe		Eselberewe	
Over and Lower Penn		Hardmead	
Rushall		Filgrove	
Bushbury		Astwode	
Great Barr		Dorton	
Perry Barr		Werseleah	
Little Barr		Tyringham	
Treshull			
Seisdon		***Dower lands of Lucy* de *Somery*** [113]	
Essington			
Himley		*Bucks:* — Newport Paganel	
Bastendon		Bradefield	
Pattingham		Soleham	
Wombourne with Overton		*Worcs:* — Oldswinford	
Mere Church		Clent Church	
		Warley	
		Staffs: — Rowley Regis Church	
		Prestwood	
		Ashwood Haye	

Lands of the Sutton Family
(That became part of the Barony of Dudley)

Cheshire
Malpas
Shokkelache
Bradeley
Ageton
Brymbelhanger
Church Christelton
Over & Nether Fulwich

Rutland
Market Overton

Derbyshire
Breydeshall
Stoke

Bedfordshire
Lynton
Lydbury
Biscote
Stoppesley
Littelgrove

Nottinghamshire
Appeltree
Aston Walls
Ekelynge
Worksop

Oxfordshire
Kingston

Essex
Theidon
Holand

Wales
Dinapowis
Lanedeane
Caldecot
Deoder

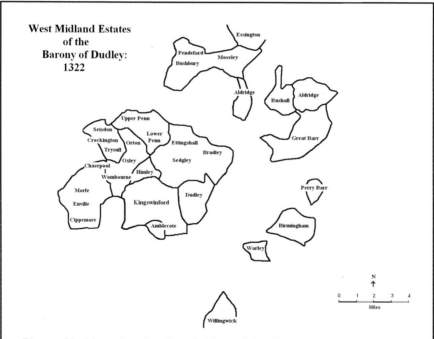

West Midland Estates
of the
Barony of Dudley:
1322

Figure 23: Map showing the division of the Barony in the in the west midlands. The barons of Dudley lost most of their Home Counties lands and some of their west midlands lands at the time of this division.

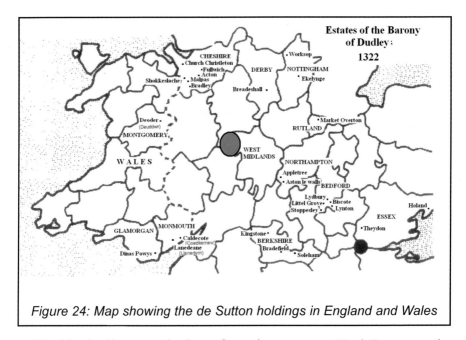

Figure 24: Map showing the de Sutton holdings in England and Wales

The king had by now raised new favourites to power: Hugh Despencer the elder, whom he had raised to Earl of Winchester, and Hugh Despencer, the younger, on whom he also lavished estates. One of these estates was in the Gower, South Wales, and by giving it to Despencer Edward was ignoring the 'Customs of the March', which had the Marcher lords in revolt. Amongst the rebels was Roger Mortimer of Wigmore, whose son had just married Margaret de Sutton's sister. Roger was captured and incarcerated in the Tower, but managed to escape by filling his gaolers with drink and then climbing down the walls with a rope. He then absconded to France. That rebellion brought the Earl of Lancaster out and King Edward used this excuse to attack his castle at Pontefract. Thomas, Earl of Lancaster was captured, quickly tried for treason and beheaded [114].

With Lancaster dead, Edward apparently had no powerful enemies, but now he seemed to be a pawn in the Despencer hands. Queen Isabella had stood the Gaveston years, now it looked as if he had been replaced by others who were far worse. Law and order began to break down even by the standards of an age that was used to violence. In March 1325 she, with her son, Edward, managed to visit her brother in France and stayed there, meeting up with Roger Mortimer, who became her lover; but the *'She wolf of France'* as she became known as, intended to come back!

Meanwhile John de Sutton was being looked at with disfavour by those in power, and in late January 1325 he was arrested in Westminster by Hugh Despencer and taken to the Marshalsea. He was charged with consorting with Humphrey de Bohun, Earl of Hereford and main supporter of Thomas, Earl of Lancaster (Bohun had been killed in battle prior to the capture and execution of Lancaster). The fact that throughout his latter years John had served with John de Somery, whom no one would ever have considered a traitor, makes the accusation absurd. But it is likely that it was not Lancaster the authorities were worried about, it was John's Marcher connections. His son was married to John de Charlton, Lord of Powys and his daughter-in-law's sister to Roger Mortimer. The barony of Dudley had been powerful under John de Somery, a royal breaker in a sea of Lancastrian supporters. If John de Sutton changed his allegiance it might have meant a collapse of royal support in the west midlands as well as the Marches. It appears that the King and the Despencers were not going to risk this. John was kept in the Marshalsea for three weeks by Simon le Croyser. On the 14th February 'in great fear of his life' he agreed to relinquish Dudley Castle and other estates to Hugh Despencer. This was what they were after; now Hugh would replace John de Somery as the king's representative at Dudley. A broken man, John was then released [115].

Hugh Despencer, 1325-1326: 15th Baron Dudley

The document to release John Sutton's estates was dated 12th October 1325 and was sealed in Chancery in Westminster. Hugh Despencer the elder got Eykeringe in Nottingham, Hugh the younger Dudley Castle, Dudley Town and the Manors of Bradefield (Berks), Duneaphowys in Wales, Seggesleye, New Swynford (Kingswinford), Rowleye Somery, (Rowley Regis), Soleham, Bastenden and Prestwode in Staffordshire [116].

Figure 25: Despencer Coat of Arms.

There is no evidence that Hugh ever came to inspect his new property, but his man on the spot was John de Botiler of Tewkesbury. His presence was discovered in the archaeological excavation in the 1980's near the castle chapel, where a tile dislaying his coat-of-arms was found.

Figure 26: Botiller Tile, found during excavation. This had been dumped during the 16th century, when John Dudley took control. It showed the coat of arms of the Botiller family, who were castle wards at the time that the Despencers usurped the barony. Source: DUCAP.

In September 1326 Queen Isabella and Roger Mortimer landed in England with an army. Support for the king melted away, and he was forced to be a fugitive in his own country. He was evenually captured in Wales in November with Hugh Despencer the younger. Edward was taken to Kenilworth Castle and Hugh to be summarily tried and executed. The French historian Jean Froissart describes Hugh's death with great relish, making a point of saying that he was castrated before he was hung till nearly dead, then taken down and drawn (his intestines taken out and burnt), and finally quartered (his arms, legs and head severed).

John de Botiler handed Dudley Castle over to the barony steward, William de Birmingham, and on the 15th December William was called to the Exchequer to surrender the castle. He put in a bill at the time for the wages he had paid out to the Castle Constable, Doorkeeper, Watchman and other estate workers (he was not paid till 1333!) [117]. Edward II relinquished his crown in January, and his son was crowned in February. On the 29th March, Henry de Bushbury, Sheriff of Stafford, was ordered to deliver up the castle to John and Margaret de Sutton. A further order to Sheriff Henry in April suggests he was enjoying the perquisites of being acting lord of Dudley and was slow at releasing it!

By this time John was heavily in debt; he had borrowed money from his son's father-in-law, John de Charlton, an amount that ran to £3,000. In a document of 1327 this was to be levied on his lands. He was also in debt to John Hildeslegh,which was levied on Malpas Castle and his lands in Cheshire. These eventually also went to John de Charlton, as did his Nottingham lands. On the 9th January 1327 his wife Margaret died and John, exhausted and broke, died soon after [118].

Figure 27: Hugh Despencer was executed in Hereford. There are a number of medieval illustrations of this event. Source: British Library.

John de Sutton II, 1327-1360: 16th Baron Dudley

John II had married Isabella de Charlton, which was just as well as the Charltons seemed to own most of the barony lands. In fact it was probably the only way in which he could recover his inheritance! In the same year that John took over the barony King Edward III, Queen Isabella and Roger Mortimer were guests of the Sutton's at Dudley Castle. But who owned what became a nightmare for John. John de Charlton, who definitely had an interest in the estate, was keen on actually running the property and in 1330 John ran foul of Joan Boteourt (his aunt), when he was accused of 'entering' her property at Sedgley. Apart from the fact that she should not have had Sedgley - it was Sutton land - Joan seems to have started a local war [119]. For some reason best known to themselves she also had the support of the local people. In the January of 1331 she and some of the prominent townsmen of Dudley 'attacked' the Castle and assaulted the castle servants. In fact they killed two Welshmen, presumably servants of Charlton - Maddock ap Yarwith and Thewelyn ap Eynon [120]. This may have just been a case of local xenophobia, but assaults continued. Hugh and John de Sutton, sons of John de Sutton of Prestwood and 32 others had carried away the Baron of Dudley's goods by force from Wolverhampton and had assaulted his men and servants and cut off their tongues and noses. A further fracas happened a few months later when Richard de Turhill of Sedgley, one of John's tenants, was also assaulted by the same men.

John II however had more important things to do than get himself involved in local squabbles. In the early 1330's he joined his father's and uncle's old comrade-in-arms Ralph Bassett and they joined King Edward III's initiative to drive the Scots from English soil. The results of this was a decisive battle fought on the 13th July 1333 in which the Scottish army was annihilated. With the Scots defeated, the French began to pressurise the English, and in 1336 the French Fleet moved into the English Channel. To the English this could only be to intimidate or attack their growing mercantile supremacy. The following year the French king confiscated Gascony and King Edward prepared for war.

In 1338 John was back at Dudley Castle when it was recorded that Simon Balle was the Castle's doorkeeper, Elias Perks the watchman and Peter was the constable. In the June of 1338 John was given permission to assart wasteland in Dudley, Sedgley, (King)Swinford and Rowley [121]. As John had to ask permission to do this, it was likely to have been land that was once a royal forest, which would in fact have been land on the edge of Pensnett Chase. The demand for more food plus the good summers of the 30's made John's assarting good agricultural sense – besides, the king's military purveyors were stock-piling grain for the coming war.

In the spring of 1340 the French were assembling a huge armada at Sluys. King Edward decided to attack it before it attacked him, so began to collect his army. John on the 28th May enfeoffed a cleric, Stephen Swetemon, to act on his behalf in his absence, and left to join the king [122]. The English fleet attacked the French fleet in the summer at Sluys and inflicted a damaging defeat on them [123]. Despite John's legal obligation to fight for the king, he is next found in the ranks of Adventurers. In 1342 Sir Walter de Manney, a Flemish soldier who came to England with King Edward's wife Phillipa de Hainult, led a force over to Brittany to relieve the siege of Hannebon. John accompanied it, but not before being summoned to attend Parliament, probably to discuss the war [124]. Another connection with Sir Walter de Manney was his involvement in holding lands of Nicholas Tewkesbury in 1343. These lands Nicholas was said to have recovered from John de Somery.

King Edward took an army to France the following year, but the French would not fight, and a truce was signed in January 1343 [125]. The king seemed pleased with John's service, as he appointed him a Justice of the Peace in 1344 and gave him the lands that John had previously leased from Walter Malet, after that knight was outlawed. The truce did not last very long, and Edward was back in France two years later and John with him. He was given letters of protection for the summer months.

John de Sutton served in the second division under the command of the Earl's of Northampton and Arundel at Crecy in 1346. His banner was not his family one, the Malpas cross, but the double lions of Dudley, the traditional standard of the barony [126]. Although the casualty figures were actually slight in the battle, the war had taken its toll over John's fighting men. At Easter 1347 John was indicted for the deaths of nearly 100 men. This was the casualty list of the war, and was a formality that the coroner had to go through.

While at home he was in a spot of bother over a debt. It appears that he had borrowed £170 from Adam de Pershale, using Himley and Swindon as security. Adam had been beheaded for rebellion and John had been slow to pay back the money to the king. He was back in France however by July, and was engaged in the Siege of Calais. He did not go unrewarded for that campaign - he was granted a number of houses and shops in that town. But there was something spreading into Europe that made the death in battle insignificant. In 1349 the Black Death arrived in England. It had a severe impact in the midlands, as it did elsewhere. The only place we have got any figures for is Halesowen, where in this year 40% of the adult males caught the disease and died [127].

Figure 28: Battle of Crecy. Source: Bibliotheque nationale.

John was summoned to Parliament in 1350, and was sent off with a relieving force to St Jean D'Angley in France, but plague was raging there as well, and for a while war took a back seat. The lesson that had been learnt in warfare was that the use of the long bow made the English virtually invincible. So it became royal policy that all males between 12 and 60 learn to use it. Archery practice became obligatory on Sunday mornings and football was banned. John was appointed in 1352 a Commissioner to Array Archers in Staffordshire.

John de Sutton concentrated on his own lands while peace held. He paid the king a ferm of £11.10.6 for Swyneford in 1352. A peculiar event happened about this time, during the voidance of the prior: John de Sutton II broke into the priory property, both at Dudley and Wodeford Grange. Goods were removed, including 6 horses, 26 oxen worth £60, spices, armour (an odd thing to have in a priory!) and two crossbows (medieval churchmen often hunted). He did not do it on his own, as according to the Patent Rolls of July 1357 he was said to have accomplices including Nicholas Jobynel Parson of Kingswinford, William Russel, William Chamberleyn, William Corbyn, William Rydere, Richard Rydere Parson of the Church of lnkpenne, William Parker, Richard Chamberleyn, Thomas Porter, Richard Bakester and others. This seems to be a who's who of the great and the good in the area around Dudley [128].

These incidents are deeply perplexing. If the honesty of John Sutton and the principal townsmen cannot be doubted, we are led to assume that they were doing it for a logical reason. The only inference that can be made is that they assumed that the Priory had come to the end of its life, and so decided to unofficially close it down by removing its belongings. Unfortunately for them a new prior turned up and was most displeased at this theft. The new prior, William de Leomestre, on the 13th July 1357 accused John de Sutton and the others of not only stealing the above mentioned goods but also breaking into the Priory and chasing and threatening to kill him. In the latter case it sounds like disappointment that they were not going to keep the priory's possessions [129].

It was ironic while all this was going on the king had given John a Commission of Justice on the 16th May 1355 relating to the Statute of Winchester and Northampton (1351) regarding labourers, artificers and servants. These Statutes gave John as a Justice of the Peace the power to fix wages and prices and control the movement of labour. The shortage of labour caused by the Black Death had resulted in the payment of wages and workers were moving to find the best paying employers. The government attempted to stamp out this very un-feudal way of doing things! [130]

The Anglo-French War resumed in 1356 - this time in Gascony. It was in this year that the Black Prince fought the Battle of Poitier. John was in his late 50's by now and was called to the colours in 1359 in the retinue of William de Bohun. King Edward led the autumn campaign against the Duke of Burgandy, in which John died less than a month after leaving England. It is not recorded whether he died of disease (common in medieval armies) or in battle. John's Inquisition Post Mortem for his lands in Worcestershire was held at Bromsgrove on 14th January 1360. Unfortunately, there is little there to tell if John, like many soldiers of his time, had made a fortune in the French Wars. His lands, as was the custom, were taken into the hands of the King's Escheator [131].

Isabella de Sutton, 1360-1397: 17th Baron Dudley

Isabella gave fealty for John's lands on his death and in February 1360, the Kings Escheator's for Worcester and Stafford delivered Dudley Castle and its estates to her despite the fact that their son John was over the age of consent - Isabella was the new Baron of Dudley. As if to prove it, a Close Roll of 26th February recorded that she and John had held the Castle jointly. Perhaps her son John had disputed her rights to the lordship.

John certainly argued about her rights of land in Kingswinford, which were actually held by Nicholas, the Parson of Kingswinford. This case went on till after the death of both litigants. Isabella was a powerful woman, with powerful friends, who according to Guttery had been a nurse to Queen Phillipa. Sometime in between 1360 and 1361 Isabella remarried - a man called Richard de Dudley. Even in the medieval period this was a little quick! A first marriage for the landed gentry was out of duty, but the second, particularly for a powerful woman as Isabella was probably out of love. Who Richard was is a mystery, the Dudley historian John Roper thought he may have been a Fisher, a very wealthy and important family in Dudley at the time [132]. Whoever he was, Isabella was marrying below her station and the rancour between herself and her son may have been partly due to this.

Richard lived nearly as long as she did, and seems to have taken over the duties of the Lord of Dudley. He was also styled as such in many documents. For instance, John de Pessali sued Sir Richard 'de Sutton' *sic* and Isabella for a third part of the manor of Himley, which she claimed was hers. It would appear that Sir Richard and Isabella were living at Himley Manor House by September 1361 [133]. Richard was licensed between 1361 and 1376 for having an Oratory there, which means they had a private chapel installed [134].

It appears that Richard and Isabella would often spend time at Halesowen Abbey. A statement of expenditure said that the Lord and Lady Dudley spent a week at the Abbey in 1366. The kitchen accounts record that they consumed: a carcase of a cow 6/-, a calf 2/1, 4/- worth of pork, a sheep costing 2/ 2, 3 suckling pigs 4/6, 10 geese 1/10½ , some herrings 5½d and 750 eggs. Some weeks before 6/8 was spent on wine for "the Lord of Weoley and his wife (the Botetourt's), the Lord Dudley and his wife, Sir Richard Fitton and his wife and the Lord Abbot of Welbeck (Welbeck was the Abbeys mother church)." [135].

Sir Richard did get involved with his JP duties; he held a commission between the years 1373 and 1380 and was categorically commissioned to seek out William Perkynnesson and others in November 1375 for running amok in Dun-Clent. Perkynnesson and the others were Dudley men. Richard

Figure 29: Eighteenth century drawing of the medieval moated Manor House at Himley.

may also have accompanied the Prince of Wales to Aquitaine. There was no fighting as this was a propaganda exercise [136]. Richard was also stated to be one of the collectors of the Staffordshire Subsidy in 1377. Richard and Isabella apparently had a son of their own called Thomas, as they left him the advowson of the Priory after Richard's death in 1383. The Prior of Dudley, Richard Wynall was one of the executors of his will together with his chaplain John Ellesmore. Richard was buried in the Carmelite Friary in Coventry. Isabella survived him till the 10th April 1397, and was buried by his side in Coventry [137].

Isabella lived a long time, and her son and grandson died before she did; thus they never became barons of Dudley. Her son John III married Catherine, daughter of the Earl of Stafford, and was living in Coleshill (Stafford land) when his son was born. They eventually moved up to the family home of Malpas Castle, where they lived for the rest of their lives.

War broke out in 1368 and John III joined John, Duke of Chandos, and the Black Prince in the following year. He may have been killed in the numerous border skirmishes of 1369 as Sir John Chandos was [138]. His son John IV was only nine when his father died, and his estates were held in wardship. Wardships were quite profitable and it was not uncommon for them to change

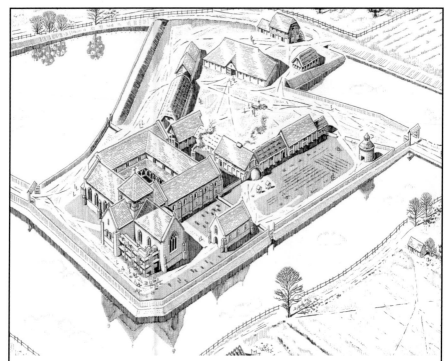

Figure 30: Reconstruction of St James' Priory, Dudley. Constance built a Lady Chapel at the Priory in remembrance of her husband John. This reconstruction shows the building work just being started. Source: DMBC Ludlow/Boland.

hands for money, as John IV's did. In 1381, Richard, Earl of Arundel and Surrey, sold the wardship to Philip le Despenser. This may have had something to do with the fact that John married Philip's daughter, Alice le Despenser, in the same year [139]. John IV was of age in 1383 and it was then that he was delivered of his father's lands of Malpas, though there was some debate about who should have held them. William de Brereton and Isabella de Egginton sued John IV for the land, who in turn sued his grandmother in 1391 [140]. War again disrupted the family household, as the now knighted Sir John de Sutton went to sea to join his old guardian, Richard, who was Admiral of England [141]. He died in 1397, though whether this was in the war or at home is unknown.

John de Sutton V, 1401-1406: 18th Baron of Dudley

John was born in 1380 and inherited the barony after his great grandmother's death and on his coming of age on 14th March 1401 [142]. John married Constance Blount, the daughter of Sir William Blount of Derbyshire, and John V was born at Barton-under-Needwood in the same year.

In the Public Record Office is a document dated 1401 and signed by Richard Beauchamp, Earl of Worcester, ordering the Constable of Dudley to *'array forces against the Welsh'* [143]. This document must be wrongly dated, as Thomas Percy was Earl of Worcester between 1401 and his execution in 1403, but he was followed in the post by Richard Beauchamp. There had been factions on the border in this period. In 1399 French forces in support of the Owain Glyndwr Rebellion held Woodbury Hill fort at Abberley, only a few miles from Dudley Castle. The French did attack Worcester in 1403, and this document may relate to that year [144]. The Welsh revolt went on until 1410, but John had died in 1406. The manner of his death is unknown. His I.P.M. was dated 16th November 1406 [145].

Constance de Sutton, 1406-1422: 19th Baron Dudley

Constance took over the Barony after her husband died. Her father, Sir William Blount of Derbyshire, had fought in Spain with John of Gaunt when he went to fight for King Peter of Castile. King Peter's daughter Constance married John of Gaunt, and one of her ladies-in-waiting, Donna Sanchia de Ayala, married William. Their daughter was named after the princess [146].

Constance got involved in baronial life, even to the extent of taking sides in family quarrels. In 1418 she was involved with Margaret Turnepeny at Brereley (Bradley near Coseley), when they sued William Turnepeny (not her husband, who was dead) for chasing 2 mares and 4 cows resulting in the death of a mare and a cow. More normal events were when she sued Elias and Frankelyn Colberne and two others of Dudley for poaching in Sedgley Park.

Although she is recorded as living at Himley, she was not always in the Midlands. In fact in a case of debt for 40/- to a London draper, no one could find her and the King took the Rectory of Kingswinford off her to pay her debts. The problem was that she had given John Bredhill (Brettell) the Rectory of Kingswinford. Being the steward and confessor of Lady Constance, he divided his time of being at his post and attending her ladyship in London or wherever she was, and he was the administrator of her estate on her death in 1432 [147].

John de Sutton VI, 1422-1487: 20th Baron of Dudley

John was born at Barton-under-Needwood in 1401 - the year his father received Dudley Castle and its estates. After her husband's death in 1406, Constance was given custody of John VI during his minority. John was styled Baron Dudley and given possession of his lands on 10th December 1422, when he came of age, although his mother, like many of the Dowager Baroness Dudley's, held on to the Lordship for her lifetime [148].

According to Grazebrook, Sir Philip Sidney in his reply to 'Leycesters Commonwealth' stated that Lord Dudley was Henry V's Lord Steward and was the King's Chief Mourner. Sir William Dugdale added to this statement that he carried the standard at King Henry V's funeral in 1422. Both Grazebrook and Dugdale assumed this to be John VI. If this were true it was a great honour for the young 21 year old. Alternatively it may have just been the case of Sidney flattering Robert Dudley, Earl of Leicester, in the 16th century by inventing another role for the great family hero [149].

In 1424 John was knighted and living in Dudley Castle as his first royal summons was sent there. He was supposedly in the retinue of the Regent of England, Humphrey Duke of Gloucester, and was given an Order of 'Protection' to go to Guynes in Northern France. The French had attempted to take back the lands in France won by Henry V and the troops who were sent out were led by the Duke of Bedford. The 'Protection' was subsequently revoked as John *'tarries in his own castle at Dudley'* [150]. Whether this was due to his mother feeling the Sutton's had not a good record of surviving French Wars, or whether he was too busy hunting, we do not know. John was a keen huntsman in the early days, and both he and John Drewet were sued for poaching in the Royal Forest of Kynfare [151].

John's next post in March 1428 was the unenviable one of Lord Lieutenant of Ireland. Why he was given it is open to question. The situation was normally considered to be only useful as a means of politically exiling great lords and members of the Royal family [152]. He appointed Nicholas Wetton, Clerk, and John Sheldon of Rowley to look after his estate while he was away and sailed for Ireland. Although the term for the post was 6 years, John did not serve that long. He was due to be paid £5,000 for the first year and £4,000 for each year after. His expenses were the pay of the soldiers he took over there. He actually received nearly a hundred per cent of the money from the English Exchequer, which was probably due to Ireland suddenly taking on a new importance. James Stewart, cousin and political opponent of King James I of Scotland, had fled to Ireland in 1425. By 1429 the English Council had realised how useful he was as a political lever against the king of Scotland,

and hoped to lure the fugitive to England. John had his work cut out to tempt him over [153].

John could have flexed his military muscle against the very independent Anglo-Irish lords, but as there was very little to gain by it, he probably accepted that his rule was confined to Dublin and the English Pale. A 'Protection' for a Dudley man to go over to Ireland was dated 28th October 1429. At the same time as John was serving in Ireland, the war with the French was reaching a crucial phase. Joan of Arc rallied the French Army in 1429, and until her death in 1431 managed to cut deep into English-held France. The English-Burgundian coalition collapsed in 1435 when the Duke of Burgundy changed sides. Without Burgundy's help the English position was untenable.

His mother Constance died in 1432 and John VI did homage and fealty for his lands. There was a problem over John Bredhill, Rector of Kingswinford, the problem being that John VI believed that he held some of his property after his mother's death. With John Sheldon of Rowley, Thomas Bradley and Thomas Yonge of Kingswinford and John, Clerk of Tipton, he paid the Rectory a visit. According to John Bredhill this occurred at Whitsun and John VI plundered his house, farm and library [154]. There seems to have been a tit-for-tat affair going on, as John VI sued John Bredhill for breaking into his houses in Kingswinford, burning them down and carrying off goods and chattels [155]. This seemed to get out of hand by 1442 when John Bredhill was indicted for:

1. Rape of Joan, wife of Reginald Tanner.
2. Accessory of robbery of silver paten from his own church.
3. For poaching in John VI's Kingswinford Park (he was caught at Barrow Hill).
4. Rape of Christine wife of John Harewood of Kyderminster and robbing him of 40 marks.

As the king subsequently pardoned him on the 10th April 1441, one can assume that at least some of these crimes were true [156].

John's other domestic problems included poaching. John Fletcher of Wolverhampton was sued in 1440 for poaching in John's wood of Wolverhampton, and Nicholas Warying, also of Wolverhampton, for poaching 200 rabbits from Himley Park.

The in-fighting of the English aristocracy that would eventually lead to the Wars of the Roses had already started by this date. Richard, Duke of York, had some of his lands confiscated by the king. John VI in this event seems to have been labelled a Yorkist, and he and others were ordered to pay 200 marks a year in two instalments at Michaelmas and Easter 1433 and 1437. These monies were as security for Richard, Duke of York's payment to the king on recovery of Richard's lands. John was also to pay at the same time £97.18.8½ and half a farthing to Humphrey, Duke of Gloucester.

When the king summoned John to the Reading Parliament in 1440, the French Wars had reached a point of crisis. It was decided a truce should be arranged, and John was one of the commissioners sent to the Court of Philip the Good, Duke of Burgundy, to make arrangements. John was rewarded for his services to the state in October 1443 by being given £100 a year out of the Petty Customs of the Port of London. The document reads:

'For good and long service to the late king and to the king in France, and Normandy and Ireland and the Marshes of Calais withoute at his great travail and cost.' [157].

John was back at home in 1446 as he signed a document at Dudley Castle in that year. King Henry VI must have had some personal experience of John VI's diplomatic capabilities, as he made him a Lord of the King's Council in 1447. The English Provinces in France were now being lost one by one. John was sent as Ambassador to treat with the Duke of Brittany in 1447 on the surrender of Maine to the French. John was also sent on a trading mission to the Court of the Duke of Burgundy two years later. Burgundy by then had managed to consolidate much of the Low Countries, and the important trading towns of Brugge, Ghent and Antwerp were now under Burgundian rule. The break between England and Burgundy had badly damaged English trading - particularly the Wool Trade. John was commissioned in 1449 to treat with King Philip in order to reopen trading relations with Flanders. In 1450 Normandy fell, and Gascony followed the next year. For all intents and purposes the Hundred Years War was now over, and all the soldiers came home.

The English defeat had a positive reaction of general dissatisfaction with the king and the government. A popular rising in Kent, led by an Irish ex-soldier called Jack Cade, marched on London with the general purpose of *'excluding the evil councillors from Henry's court'*. In June 1450 John VI was given a commission to suppress Cade's Rebellion, which he successfully did. Popular discontent still existed however, and local jurors charged John with taking horses and money during the 'campaign' (possibly petty pilfering by his retainers?) - something one would not have expected if they had been avid supporters of the king [158].

From 1450 onwards, however, King Henry VI's problem was not the people but his own feuding aristocracy. His cousin, Richard Duke of York, who could have been considered to be an heir to Henry's crown, was isolated by Henry's favourites, the Lancastrian Dukes of Somerset and Suffolk. Richard was sent to Ireland as Lord Lieutenant in 1449 (the same job as John VI had done in 1428). On Cade's Rebellion in 1450 Richard raced back with an army. Although the rebellion was quashed, Richard had no intention of returning to Ireland and in 1451 he took up arms against the Government. His argument was, like that of Cade, he merely wanted to get rid of the King's 'evil councillors'. What he in fact did was start the civil war known ever since as the Wars of the Roses.

John VI was on the King's business in Gloucester when the war started and was immediately arrested by Richard and sent to Ludlow Castle as a prisoner. Richard met King Henry and the King promised that he would include some of the Duke of York's friends in the Council, but refused to get rid of his own appointed barons. John VI was shown to be a councillor in a petition of 1451 laid before parliament [159]. John was freed and Henry appointed him to the post of Treasurer of the King's Household, an extremely lucrative position. It was as Treasurer that in 1453 John became keeper of the lands in Glamorgan, which were in dispute by the Dukes of York and Somerset [160].

The enmity between the York and Lancaster factions was just waiting to erupt into open warfare, and when Henry went insane in the middle of 1453, it broke out again. Richard took over the mantle of power and had Somerset committed to the Tower of London. When the king regained his senses in December, Richard and his powerful allies, the Earls of Salisbury and Warwick, were dismissed, and Somerset was released [161]. One of King Henry's greatest supporters was his Queen, Margaret of Anjou. She lived in a very grand scale indeed as can be seen when John VI was responsible for her expenses in 1452-1454. A bill of £797.8.11½ was paid just for her food, it was stated to be:

'for the diet of Margaret lately called Queen' [162]

Richard, Duke of York, did not take this dismissal lying down, and declared war on the King. The two sides met at St. Albans on 22nd May 1455. John VI was at the King's side, and was wounded in the face by an arrow during the battle. The king's forces were routed and John took refuge in the cathedral. He was found however and taken to the Tower by the Yorkists [163]. Presumably he would have concluded that this was preliminary to his execution. In the Paston Letters, there is correspondence from William Barker, a Londoner to William Worcester, Secretary to Sir John Fastolf, dated June 1455.

'The Baron Dudley is in the Tower; what shall come of him godwot. ' [164].

John Sutton was too good a diplomat to remain in the Tower for long, and Richard released him and commissioned him to go to France in order to arrange a marriage between Magdalena (family presently unknown) and his son Edward. Nothing eventually came of the mission [165]. The peace, however, was not to last long, and King Henry began to build up his own Lancastrian faction. In 1459 he again called a Great Council, which met at Coventry. The Dukes of York, Salisbury and Warwick were not invited! They replied in the by now traditional way - they raised an army! The Battle of Blore Heath on 23rd September 1459 was a victory for Henry. John, however, faced the ignominy of again being wounded and captured. He was well rewarded for his faithfulness however, as Henry made him a Knight of the Garter [166].

Although Richard of York's fortunes rose at the beginning of the following year, he and Salisbury were killed in battle near Sandal Castle in Yorkshire. The Yorkist's, not to be outdone, crowned Richard's son Edward (IV), and defeated the Lancastrians in battle on the 29th March 1461 at Towton, also in Yorkshire [167]. John VI seems to have changed sides at this time, as the Earl of Warwick sent him off to France on another diplomatic mission in 1460. On 8th July 1461 King Edward IV issued a Commission of Peace; John, amongst other important barons, is named on it [168].

King Edward rewarded John with 100 marks from the Duchy of Cornwall and £100 per annum from the Great and Petty Customs of the Port of Southampton in 1465. John was also allowed to trade in wool (at the cheap customs duty of 4 marks a sack) from the Ports of London, Sandwich and Southampton to any port abroad including the *'Straits of Marrock'* (Morocco). He was also allowed to bring back any merchandise including *'bullin in mass or in plate of gold and silver to change and mint'*. It looks as if John did not always get what was his due out of the Customs Service, as the Port of Southampton was ordered to pay £100 in arrears in January 1484 [169].

Although we have no evidence to support it, John VI may also have been involved in the Anglo-French Treaty of 1463, brought about no doubt through John's previous diplomatic experience with the Dukes of Burgandy. John was granted the Manor of Bordesley in 1466. A later alliance with Burgundy in 1468 could also involved John. John had a number of guests at Dudley Castle, as Henry Beaumont was recorded as staying there on 4th July 1467 [170].

With the Earl of Warwick's ambitions of power, the War of the Roses however was far from dead. He rebelled against King Edward in 1471, and with French support put King Henry back on the throne. John's son Edward had married the Earl of Worcester's daughter - the Earl was killed at this time. King Edward was not going to loose his throne so easily, and met the Earl of Warwick in battle at Barnet on 13th March 1471. Warwick the kingmaker not only lost the battle but also his life. King Edward had King Henry murdered, and for a while peace reigned. Edward did not bear malice however, and allowed many Lancastrians the chance to start or continue their careers in his service. John VI was appointed to be one of the envoys involved in a marriage treaty between Princess Cecilia and James, son of King James of Scotland [171].

In 1473 he was given the important post of Constable of the Tower of London. If he was still Constable in 1478, the imprisoned Duke of Clarence was murdered by being drowned in a huge barrel or butt of Malmsey Wine while in his charge. The document of appointment suggests that John's deputy, Anthony Lord Rivers, for two payments of £100 per annum, could appoint his own officers and receive all wages and profits. Therefore it is possible that the day to day running of the state prison was little to do with John. The King's Treasurer (and others) appear to have paid a bond of £1,000 on John's appointment.

King Edward now turned to his 'natural' enemy, France, and with Burgundian support invaded France in 1475. This came to nothing and a peace treaty between the two powers was signed at Picquigny in the same year. A Dudley document cites John as being one of the Commissioners at the truce, but as it is dated 1477 it may be wrongly dated, as France and England were not at war in that year.

Now in his 70's, John VI seems to have contented himself with home affairs. He sued John Wodehouse of Albrighton, yeomen, for breaking into his close and houses at Himley and taking 300 sheep worth 40 marks and other goods and chattels to the value of 20 marks [172]. In 1483 he re-acquired the old Somery manors of Northfield and Weoley. After the Great Fire of Dudley in 1476 it seems likely that the Church of St Edmunds had suffered by having its chancel burnt down. In 1485, (the year of the Battle of Bosworth), John was rewarded for 'services to the realm' by being made Steward of the Forest of Kinver. He used this position to acquire 60 oaks from the Royal Forest to give to the townsmen of Dudley so that they could rebuild their chancel and Lady Chapel [173]. A great benefactor of the Lady Chapel was his son William Dudley, who was Dean of the Household of King Edward IV and later Bishop of Durham [174]. John also had an annex built next to the keep as an extra kitchen.

Sir John Sutton, Knight of the Garter, Baron Dudley and Malpas, died on the 15th October 1487. He instructed that his body was to be buried in the Priory of Dudley and that a tomb of the value of £20 be erected over his body [175]. John was one of the longest lived of the Barons of Dudley in a age when intrigue or war killed aristocrats off early. He survived not because he was a great soldier, but because he was a great diplomat, a professional 'civil servant' who bridged the gap between the divided houses of York and Lancaster.

Edward Sutton I, 1487-1532: 21st Baron of Dudley

Edward I was born in 1459, the year his grandfather fought at Blore Heath. His father was John IV's eldest son Edmund Sutton, who had died before his grandfather, and his mother was Joice Tiptoft, daughter to the Earl of Worcester and Constable of England. Edward's earliest official engagement was when he was 26. This was on the 25th November 1485, when he was knighted at the Coronation of Elizabeth of York, wife to Henry Tudor of Lancaster, the seventh king of that name. Edward became Baron of Dudley two years later on his grandfather's death in 1487.

At first things seemed to go well with Edward, but in the middle 1490's he had an Act of Attainment brought against him. The reason at the present is unknown. However, this was the period when Perkin Warbeck claimed himself to be Richard Duke of York, son of King Edward VI. Richard and his brother had been incarcerated in the Tower of London after the death of their father. They were never seen again! Warbeck was in Burgundy in 1496 being 'wined and dined' by its ruler Maximillian, and talk was put abroad that Burgundian and other continental support might be found to oust King Henry VII off the English throne.

Early in 1495 King Henry had everyone suspected of supporting the 'impostor' arrested. Perhaps Edward was imprisoned at the time. The Sutton's friendship with the Burgundian court may have given rise to suspicion. In July 1495, the De Facto Act made anyone who physically supported the King against Warbeck automatically innocent of treason, but it was Sir William Berkeley, one of the king's close supporters, who eventually managed to get Edward's attainment annulled in 1496. Tied in with the attainment was the Grant of Northfield and Weoley to the King's uncle, the Duke of Bedford. It is not likely that Edward was the instigator of the grant, as in 1496 he managed to get it made null and void.

Edward I's relations with his sovereign improved after this date. He was invited to attend the Parliaments of 1497 and 1504 and married Cicely, the daughter of Sir William Willoughby. The king gave him the wardship of John, son of John Grey, Lord of Powis, who died in 1496. Edward was granted custody of Kereign and other places in Wales belonging to the Greys. He was given another wardship in 1502, that of Edward de Birmingham. This he sold to Edward's mother, who passed it on to William Coningsby. Edward de Birmingham was to prove a future problem to his one-time guardian however.

Edward I was again in trouble with the authorities in 1503, when he was tried for a felony by the Earl of Surrey, Lord High Steward of England [176]. The details of this second brush with the law are no more clear than the first, but this was the period that King Henry was cracking down on the retinues of powerful barons through his Statute of Liveries. It was another of the king's legal reforms that led to the reassessment of Edward's wardships in 1504. He was to pay a £1,000 recognizance and £50 per year to the Crown for Grey's property. The source of many of these money making schemes for the King was Edward's own cousin, Edmund Dudley. He and the King's lawyers had been busy scrutinising every ancient document they could find (including Magna Carta) in order to find out what levies could be made against the baronies. Further debts to the king were recorded against Edward in 1508.

King Henry VII died in the April of 1509 and his son Henry VIII was crowned. The reigns of the Tudors brought about many changes to aristocratic life, but those families that had survived the Wars of the Roses and Henry VII's taxes could relax a little during the reign of his son. There was a tendency to want to be close to the King's Court, ostensibly to join in the fun, but in reality because that was where the posts and perquisites could be obtained. In 1509 Edward borrowed money from John Barel. This may have been to pay for the Coronation Ceremony, when he was made a Knight of the Garter, but in 1511 he was still a debtor to the king. Without an increase in income he was not going to get out of the ever increasing spiral of debt. His cousin Edmund Dudley had tried to help him when he bought a marriage conveyance for one of Edward's daughter in June 1509. The husband to be was William Clyfford, Son of Charles Clyfford, one of Edmund's debtors. Edmund Dudley however was executed, as his services to the previous crown had been described as over zealous. An annuity of £20 from the Grey's lands was given to Edward's brother John in 1516. In reality it looks as if he could not even afford to keep this wardship. By 1517 Edward owed the King such large sums in back rents that a warrant was issued in the May cancelling his recognizances and pardoning him for his debts - the wardship went back to the King!

As everything was happening in London, Edward rented a house in Tothill Street, Westminster, in 1522. From that date on the Sutton family considered London to be their second home. Edward was back at Dudley Castle in 1525 as he signed a document there, but his finances were still deteriorating. By the late 20's he was forced into selling parts of his property, the Sutton families' most important estate - the Castle and Manor of Malpas. This went to a George Robinson in 1527. The Priory of Sandwell was offered to the king's Royal Chancellor, Cardinal Thomas Wolsey, in the same year. The property was to go to the Dean and Canons of Wolsey's newly founded University College of Oxford. According to a document of 1526, there was some discrepancy about the rents before it was given to Wolsey.

Edward seems to have known Wolsey quite well. A letter survives written by him from Dudley Castle in January 1529, referring to young Edward de Birmingham, who seems to have degenerated into a 'tearaway' and was resorting to robbing people in the west midlands area:

"Most reverent ffader in God; and my most especial good lorde, in my most lowly wyse I recommand me unto your good Grace. Please it the same your grace to have knolege that uppon the nyght afore Christmas eveyn last passed; on Edward Byrmingham and to off his servants, whose names be Robert Sutton and Henry Fox, with in a myle of my castell off Dudleye, in the Counte of Staff, beytt woundyd and robyd a tenent of myn of Dudley whoes name is John Moseley, and toke from hymm iiij. viij off money, and laught hym for dede and whot swit fouoloid after and toke them in Schropsheyre with the maynonok and aftorwards by on Ruff of Warley, and other conveyed them into Wiscettorschyre, to the intent that they by the heipe of ther frends may come unto their Asquytall. On of the thevys whoes name is Henry Fox confessid and seid that ther was a hundred persons thyvs of their affynite and company within three scheyrs adoining, and now the said Edward Byrmyngham and off his seid to servants make no dowt butt the woll obteyn and gett ther pdon. of the Kyng's Grace and off your Grace in consideracon wher of it myght pleise your grace to sent for the said Edward Byrmyngham and his to seruauntts to the intent that they may be examyned that ther affynyte of this nounbor off thevys myght be knowen and taken. Your Grace shall doe a gracious deide as well for quyatacion of the King's subgette, as a vodying of such robberys and murder as hathe be done a bowte the towne of Byrmyngham, as knoweth the xxiiii day of Januarii.

And if it may please your said L Grace to her this berer speke he shall showe his Grace forther of my mynde, which I trust your Grace wolbe content withall. More worthe to youe then the Priory of Sondewell that I yeve youe to your Newe Colege of Oxforde.

Your jumbyell orator Edward Dudley

To the most reverent father in God the lord Legate Cardinal Archbishop of Yorke, Chauncellor and Primate Metropolitan of England. This to be delivered in goodly hast." [177]

As can be seen, spelling was not one of Edward's accomplishments! The 'young' de Birmingham was caught and convicted in 1536, and the King confiscated his manor.

Edward's ever decreasing financial situation seems to have forced him into selling Northfield in 1531. He died on the 31st January in the following year. His I.P.M. taken in 1533 stated that the town of Dudley was valued at £10. The Castle and foreign of Dudley plus Netherton was 5 marks [178].

John Sutton VII, 1532-1537: 22nd Baron of Dudley

John was born in 1496. His earliest documentary reference was in 1509, when he was bound with his father to a loan from John Barel - a poor start which some how set the seal on the rest of his life's activities! John is supposed to have been knighted in 1513 in France, which may mean he was with Henry VIII's unsuccessful invasion force. He was unfortunate to have been the son of a far from wealthy aristocrat at a time of rising inflation. In order to keep up the standards of his position, he borrowed money heavily prior to becoming Lord Dudley. These loans were no doubt given on the understanding they would be paid back when he inherited his estate [179]. John married Cicely Grey, the daughter of Thomas Grey, Marquis of Dorset, at this time. The Dudley name became inextricably tied with the Greys. As well as his own connection, his cousin, Guilford Dudley, married Lady Jane Grey, John's niece.

When his father died in 1532 and at the age of 36, John became the new Baron Dudley. His creditors immediately closed in on him. He needed a lot of money and fairly quickly. The only way out was to mortgage his estates, and it was to his cousin John Dudley he went. A number of other men were involved in the mortgage, which amounted to £4,200, but it was John Dudley who had a personal interest in it.

John Sutton's Creditors

George, 4th Earl of Shrewsbury	Held State offices
Sir Thomas West, 9th Lord La Ware	Soldier and courtier
Thomas Fitzalyn, Lord Maltravers	
William Whorwood	Attorney General to King Henry VIII

Sir Edward Seymour, Earl of Hertford
Thomas Arundell, Privy Councillor (Wolsey)
George Carewe Courtier
Thomas Wyatt Poet, Privy Councillor (Henry VIII)
Andrew Dudley (Sir John Dudley's brother) [180]

£2,000 of this sum was said to have been borrowed from John Dudley through his brother Andrew, and it was paid back at £400 a year. It is more likely that there were in fact two mortgages, and it seems certain that John Sutton quickly began to regret letting his ambitious cousin get a part hold on the family's ancestral lands. In the same year as the loan he wrote to Thomas Cromwell (Cromwell had replaced Wolsey as the King's close advisor), begging him to use his influence with the King to persuade him to pay the £2,000 back to Sir John Dudley and take the Manor of Sedgley, worth £180 per annum, for 20 years. In his letter John stated that he was afraid to go to London because:

"Sir John Dudley lays wait for me... ..to keep me afore the days of payment." [181]

Cromwell seems to have ignored the request, as John wrote again in the following year. Cromwell must have agreed to a loan at some time as John is recorded in a Close Roll of 1538 to be in debt to him for the sum of £1,000. In so quickly mortgaging his estate John had conveniently forgotten that his mother had a claim on it as part of her dowery. These included Sedgley, Himley, Rowley Regis, Kingswinford, Prestwood, Oxley and Dudley-Netherton. The Dowager Lady Dudley wrote to Sir Thomas Audley, the Lord Chancellor, in 1533, complaining about her son's actions. John was summoned to the Court of Exchequers in 1534 and pleaded that

He was compelled to borrow money in his father's lifetime and that he needed to mortgage his lands to become solvent - besides which he could not find the documents referring to his mother's lands. [182]

The Court was more interested in whether or not alienating baronial lands held in trust for the king was an offence. It was stated that Sir Andrew Dudley received the right to the premises but Sir John Dudley still held the demesne. Presumably this did not contravene the law. As for Lady Dudley, nothing appears to have been done about her claim to her lands.

John was not the only person having financial problems - so was the King! Thomas Cromwell, as an aid to staving off royal bankruptcy, hit upon the idea of dissolving the monasteries in the mid 1530's. These church estates were very valuable, and this money would all go into the royal coffers. On February 10th 1535 Cromwell wrote to the Prior of Dudley requesting that they had a meeting regarding the preliminaries to the dissolution of St James Priory, Dudley. The Official Receiver, Richard Lee, took over Wenlock Priory and its cell Dudley Priory in 1539 [183].

Unfortunately geting rid of his debts was not so easy for John, and he was unable to pay back the loans. Sir John Dudley, being the major shareholder in John Sutton's debts, purchased the castle and the bulk of the baronial estate. According to the Victoria County History for Worcestershire, this was in 1535, but a document in the State Papers dated 23rd May 1537 suggests that it was at this date the lands were sold. The middle man was Roger Brown, a mercer of London, and the lands were to go to 'Sir John Dudley of Sussex'. Lord Shrewsbury and partners still held the other part of the estate as stated in a document of 1538.

The division of the barony was as such:

Lands of Sir John Dudley
Dudley Castle, Sedgley, Ettingshall, Woodsetton, Upper Gornal, Nether Gornal, Briereley (Bradley), Coseley, Darlaston, Ettingshall End, Gospel End, Perton.
Lands of the Earl of Shrewsbury and Others
Rowley Regis, Himley, Kingswinford, Wombourne, Swindon, Yardley, Pen, Dudley Town, Netherton and various Woods.

Sir John Sutton was now destitute. Although he did retain his house in London, for the most part he spent the remaining 18 years of his life wandering from one benefactor to another. This habit resulted in him being given the nickname 'Lord Quondam' (Lord Wants). His family were in the same dire straits. His wife Cicely and one of his daughters sought refuge in Nuneaton Priory where they were given *'meat and drink free of costs.'* [184].

John died in September 1553 and was buried in St. Margaret's Church, Westminster. Grazebrook describes his funeral, which was apparently very grand. His wife Cicely died on the 28th April in the following year. She was buried near her husband in St Margaret's.

John Dudley, 1537-1553: 23rd Baron of Dudley

John was born in 1502, the eldest son of Edmund Dudley. Due to the fact that he appeared to have usurped the family lands, it was a regular contention that his family were in fact descended from humble carpenters of the town of Dudley, but this was not the case. John's grandfather was the second son of John Sutton VI, also named John, who had married Elizabeth Bramshot of Sussex, and the family subsequently hailed from that county [183].

His father, Edmund Dudley, was a lawyer who specialised in finance. As one of King Henry VII's financial 'whiz-kids', he helped to relieve the aristocracy of their money, the legality of which was sometimes debateable. He was thoroughly detested, and when King Henry died, Henry VIII did nothing to protect him from the assaults of his enemies. In 1510 Edmund was attainted and beheaded - a not very auspicious start for young John!

After his father was imprisoned in 1509, John was made a ward of Sir Edward Guilford. Guilford seems to have been a good man, and managed to get Edmund's attainder lifted postumously in 1511, and John had his father's property restored to him. In 1520, the year of the 'Field of the Cloth of Gold', he married his guardian's daughter, Jane Guilford. John spent much of his earlier life at the Court of Henry VIII. He was described as *'an elegant and accomplished courtier who had a charming personality'* [186]. He was also a first class athlete who was considered to be one of the finest jousters of his day. As the King also considered himself to be a talented jouster, John became very popular where it mattered.

Figure 32: Contemporary Portrait of Sir John Dudley. National Portrait Gallery, London.

War broke out between England and France in 1521. In 1523 John accepted a lieutenancy in Charles Brandon, Duke of Suffolk's, expedition against King Frances. He did well, and his services to the crown resulted in a knighthood. For most of the 1520's and early 30's he was consolidating his position at court. This resulted in him raising 200 men and serving with the Duke of Norfolk in the Pilgrimage of Grace uprising in 1536. He was then appointed vice-admiral of a small fleet to combat piracy emanating from Flanders. In the same year he was appointed the king's Chief Trencher Bearer.

John seems to have acquired the Dudley estates of his cousin in 1537 as he wrote a letter about this time from Dudley stating that he had *'come home to Dudley'*. Two years later he rented Dudley Priory off the Crown for a yearly rent of £37.0.9. (In actual fact he did not pay the rent and was sued for arrears totalling £185.3.9 in 144.) John did not keep all his lands, as he sold Perton to James Leveson of Wolverhampton for £400 in 1540 [187].

It seems highly unlikely that John Sutton handed his castle over cheerfully to John Dudley, and evidence of his attitude might be implied in that John got his brother Arthur Dudley to remove *'charters, writings, court rolls, rentals and terriers'* from *'certain chests and coffers being in the said castle'*. Arthur Dudley was a priest, a prependary of Lichfield, and at the time of the Dissolution he also took the bones of St Chad kept in that Cathedral. (For a short while they were with the Bradley's at High Arcal, Woodsetton, though now they are kept in St Chad's Roman Catholic Cathedral in Birmingham.) Without the documentation, the transfer must have been difficult, and Sir John Dudley wrote to Sir Thomas Audley in 1538 complaining about it [188].

John Dudley was created Viscount Lisle in 1541. This title came from his mother's family, and in the same year he was made Warden of the Scottish Marches. The fact that ten years later he was also created Duke of Northumberland was probably based on his work in the Marches.

In 1543 King Henry began to plan another war with France. John by now was an important adviser to the king and he was created High Admiral in the January. On St Georges Day of the same year he was made a Privy Councillor and Knight of the Garter. In July of the following year an English Army landed in Calais and Bolougne was captured by the 18th of September. The commander of the forces was the Duke of Norfolk, and his organisation of supplies was hopeless, so it was up to John Dudley to speed up deliveries to the continent. These were so successful that John managed to get ships crossing twice a day, and the army were delivered from starvation. John's handling of the crisis made him very popular.

In 1545 the French gathered an Armada of 235 ships and sailed into the Solent 'to liberate England from the Protestant tyranny that Henry VIII had imposed on them'. John gathered together a fleet of 40 large warships and requisitioned 100 merchantmen to muster at Portsmouth. On the 15th July King Henry joined him, and on the evening they dined on the flag ship Henry Grace a Dieu (The Great Harry) with other senior captains. The next day they went out to fight the French. John Dudley placed the ships in line abreast with only a few cannon pointing at the enemy, which meant they had to turn to fire. One of the ships, the Mary Rose, fired a broadside and then 'came about' to fire one from the other side. As she turned she heeled over and sank. Only 40 of the 700 crew survived.

Although the French landed on the Isle of Wight, the invasion failed, and on the 28th July the French Fleet withdrew, but was later defeated off Shoreham. The invasion was a costly fiasco, and the Peace Treaty of Amiens was greeted by both sides when it was signed the following year.

Figure 32: Engraving of the Solent Battle, 1545. The sinking of the Mary Rose can be made out in this contemporary illustration. Presumably John Dudley is one of the men watching the event. Source: Mary Rose Trust.

Figure 33: Pewter Plate with the Garter Arms of John Dudley. These plates were recovered from the wreck in the recent excavation. Perhaps they were given to the various officers by John Dudley as a souvenir of the presumed coming victory the night before the battle. Copyright Mary Rose Trust.

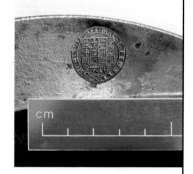

Henry VIII was now very ill, and realising that his imminent death was going to cause a political vacuum, the Seymour brothers, Thomas and Edward, pushed themselves into the foreground of the Privy Council. Their first move was to have Norfolk condemned for ineptitude and treason in December 1546. King Henry died a month later, leaving his nine year old son, Edward, to be supervised by a Regency Council. John Dudley was one of the 16 executors of this body. Edward was crowned king on the 28th January 1546-7. The Council then elected Edward Seymour (Duke of Somerset) to be Lord Protector of the king. It seems likely that the Seymours were attempting to 'crowd' John Dudley out, and he was forced into giving up his post of Lord Admiral to Thomas Seymour. John took it badly, and began to plot the downfall of the two brothers. He did not lose out completely however, as in February 1547 he was created Earl of Warwick and Chamberlain for life. He was styled in one contemporary document as 'Earl of Warwick, Viscount Lisle, Baron de Somery and Tyas and Lord of Dudley.'

Some time after acquiring Dudley Castle John had decided to convert the medieval building into a more modern style. The architect he selected was Sir William Sharrington. Sharrington had bought Laycock Abbey after the Dissolution, and started to convert it into a home in 1540. Sir William was made Vice-Treasurer of the Bristol Mint in 1546, and began counterfeiting and clip-

Figure 34: Computer image of the Sharrington Range in the 1550's.
Source: Colin Johnson, Image Interactive.

ping coins. This was often done as a perquisite of the job, but not in the manner that Sir William did it, and his profits ran into many thousands of pounds. Needless to say he was caught, and in 1548 he was arrested on a charge of high treason - currency fraud was a capital offence in England. During his hearing William stated that much of the money had gone to Thomas Seymour. Meanwhile Thomas was occupied with his own treasonable offences by attempting to court Princess Elizabeth, abduct King Edward, and by planning a coup against his brother. He was arrested, attainted and beheaded in 1549.

Meanwhile Sharrington, who had also been attainted, and whose lands were forfeit to the king, was now pardoned. His fortunes rose so high that he was able to buy back Lacock for £8,000, and continued to work there. The important question was how had he got away with it, and the answer must have been - John Dudley! John was waiting for Thomas to do something wrong, and by Sir William 'turning states evidence' against him it was just what he wanted. It is a possibility Sharrington was part of a well planned plot against Thomas Seymour, and it was understood that his offences real or contrived would be automatically pardoned. Besides which, Sir William had also shown interest in re-designing Dudley Castle, and he could not do that if he had been hung, drawn and quartered.

John Dudley now only had Edward Seymour to deal with, and as before, events seemed to go his way. In 1549 the Tudor Enclosures were starting to affect the small farmers. The hardest hit were in Norfolk, and it was here that a rebellion occurred, led by Robert Kett. Seymour seemed to be ineffectual, and John raised an army, and by September had put the revolt down. He was severe but not brutal, and when asked why he had hanged so few he replied *"Shall we hold the plough ourselves, play the carter and labour the ground with our own hands!"* [189]. Edward Seymour's star now waned, and he was beheaded for treason in 1552.

Despite the fact that most of the time his work kept him well away from Dudley, John still kept in touch with his midland estates. He asked Walter Wrottesley in a letter of 18th February 1552 to help in a survey of the Manor of Sedgley.

"To my cosen, Walter Wrotisley, esquier, this be given: Cozen Wrotisley:-
I artilly recommende me unto you, and whereas I do perceyve by my serv-
ant, Henery Cresset, that you can be content to take some paynes for me in
the surveying of my landes, I will deserve the same paynes that ye shall
therein take if it lye in me.
Mr Willoughby, that us of my consaill, is appointed to mete with you at

Dudeley the fryrst Sundaye of Lente, where I praye you not to faile to mete hym, and he shall nowe receyve a patent of £4 a yere, growing out of my lordship of Seggisley, in recompense of your old patent of v. marks a yere, and this I commyt you to God; aft the Courte this xviiith daye of Februarye. Yours loving kinsman assuredly John Duddeley." [190]

John Dudley was made Lord Protector in 1552, and now was the most powerful man in England. The young King Edward saw his new guardian as some sort of hero, and was no more happier than being in his company, either outdoors hunting (John was a skilled bowman) or being told stories about John's deeds in the past. King Edward kept a diary, and under the heading January 3rd 1551 he recorded a tournament with John Dudley, Earl of Warwick, leading the 'Chalengours' and a number of other Lords being the 'Defendours' [191].

At the same time as Sharrington was back in circulation, John commissioned John Shute to go to Italy to study architecture. The drawings he sent back to England were perused for hours by the Lord Protector and the king, who were both interested in the new Renaissance building style. Whether Sharrington saw any of these drawings and used ideas from them for Dudley Castle is not known. In 1553 Sharrington wrote a letter to Sir John Thynne (Edward Seymour's right-hand man, who had retired to his country house of Longleat after the Duke's fall to continue building it in the new style). This letter suggested that the work at Dudley Castle was coming to an end and that his mason, John Chapman, would be moving to Longleat after he had finished at Dudley. Chapman was known to have worked on a number of Henry VIII's buildings, and was strongly influenced by the French and Italian styles.

In 1551 John reorganised the Regency Council and made himself Earl Marshall of England. He was also created Duke of Northumberland. John was now extremely busy, and it was just as well he *'niether drank nor gamed'*, but ill health was starting to let him down. One of his wisest moves was to employ the very capable Sir William Cecil (later Lord Burleigh) to be his secretary. During this period one of his most famous legislations was the closing down of the Chantries in 1551; ostensibly this was to appeal to the strong growth of Protestanism in the country, but in fact John realised what large revenues would flow into the empty treasury - England was bankrupt again! During the excavations in the Great Chamber of Dudley Castle, numerous floor tiles from the chapel were discovered dumped on the floor. This seemed to show that John's Protestantism was very real, as this was done in his period, and it signified a change from the decorated Roman Catholic layout of the chapel to the new plain look.

It is hard to imagine John being short of money, so one assumes his pardon on 15th January 1552 for debts and arrears for the rent of Dudley Priory was an oversight on his part. In fact John had a number of homes to think about apart from Dudley Castle. There were three London Palaces; Durham House in The Strand, Ely Palace in Holborn and Sion House at Isleworth. John Dudley also realised that England had great potential in trading as a world power, and founded a joint stock company for exploration overseas; its navigator was Sebastian Cabot. In the latter part of the century, under men like Hawkins, Drake and Raleigh, this would come to fruition.

By 1553 the king had contracted TB and it was obvious he was going to die. John, in an effort to control the succession, had the king make the princesses Mary and Elizabeth's rights to the throne void, and put Lady Jane Grey, a cousin, next in line. To add to his security, he arranged the marriage of his youngest son, Guilford Dudley, to Lady Jane. The wedding took place on 21st May at his home of Durham House. King Edward died on the 6th July, and Lady Jane Grey was proclaimed Queen and moved to the Tower two days later. Princess Mary learnt about the event on the 9th July, and suddenly found herself with the full support of the Norfolk and Suffolk gentry. John quickly raised an army of 6,000 foreign mercenaries and marched out of London on the 14th July, but as he left the city he had heard the fleet had mutinied against him. Like his father, he had made many enemies on his rise to power, and five days later a coup d'etat occurred against him in the Privy Council. John was at Cambridge when he was told to proclaim Mary queen. This he did on the 20th July. They then ordered his arrest and he was brought back to London with Princess Mary. They both resided in the Tower - but different parts!

John was arraigned at Westminster Hall for Treason on the 18th August and executed on Tower Hill in front of a crowd of 10,000 at 10 am on the 22nd August 1553. No Lord of Dudley had ever been, nor ever would become, so powerful again!

Edward Sutton II, 1554-1586: 24th Baron of Dudley

Edward was the eldest son of John Sutton, the 22nd Baron Dudley. It probably seemed likely to him that when his father lost Dudley Castle and the lands of the Barony to John Dudley in the 1530's he would never inherit the lordship, and therefore would need a career. It may be with this in mind that he joined his uncle's retinue in Ireland in 1536. His uncle, Lord Leonard Grey, was Deputy Lieutenant, and was in the process of suppressing the Irish Catholics. Edward was captain of a company of archers under the command of Sir William Brereton (Brereton's total force was 250 men) [192].

When he returned to England, like his father Edward approached Thomas Cromwell for his advances, and although the king's chief minister seemed interested in him, nothing came of it. Edward's poverty also lost him a potential marriage to the widowed Lady Berkeley, ward to the king, circa 1540. He therefore continued with his military career, and joined the English forces in Henry VIII's last French War. He was recommended with his brother in Sir William Paget's despatches to Lord Petre (Secretary of State) for *forwardness in service'* in 1545. He remained in France for the next few years, and in 1547 served under Lord Grey in the Council of Boulogne. In the same year he spent part of his salary on the town's defences [193].

He returned to England in the first year of Queen Mary's reign, and was knighted after her coronation in October 1553. A Scottish war was then brewing, so he joined the campaign and was made Governor of Hume Castle. On Northumberland's death in 1553, Dudley Castle and estates were taken into the hands of the crown. A document of 6th September 1553 shows that John Littleton of Frankley was made Constable of Dudley Castle and Ranger of the Old and New Parks for life [194]. But by 1554 the Castle and estates were returned to Edward Sutton in three grants. Two parts (including the castle) for a service of one knights fee and the third part for an annual rent to the Exchequer of £12.5s.8d [195].

Grant 1: Dudley Castle, Conigree, Old Park, Rowley Regis.

Grant 2: Sedgley, Kingswinford, Himley, Ashwood, Chasepool, Wombourne and Swindon.

Grant 3: Dudley, Dudley Priory, Netherton Cradley, Harbourn, Treshull and the Tithes of Northfield and Sedgley.

As there was some debate with Sir John Littleton over the park and castle, Edward agreed to hold it jointly with him, and to pay a yearly rent of £80. This was to revert to the survivor. On the 4th November 1554, Edward was summoned to the House of Lords as Baron of Dudley, and attended parliament from this date till 1576 [196]. Edward seems to have attracted the attention of Queen Mary, and he was given permission to marry one of the Queen's favourite gentlewomen, Katherine Bridges, daughter of Lord Chandos of Sudeley Castle. As Katherine, as well as the Queen, was of the Roman Catholic faith, it is possible that Edward was too. This might also explain the suspicion that the following monarch, Queen Elizabeth, had about him.

In 1558 Queen Mary died, and Elizabeth came to the throne. Edward was on active service in the Lowlands at the time and had been given command of Hampness Castle in Picardy. A surprise French attack saw the fall of Guisnes, leaving Hampness the only castle left to stop the French advance towards the coast. Unfortunately Edward's decision to abandon Hampness was construed as less than proper conduct, and his military career seems to have come to an end.

His wife Katherine died in April 1566, and she was buried at St Edmunds, Dudley. Edward remarried in 1567 to Jane Stanley, daughter of the Earl of Derby. She died after the birth of their second son in 1569 and was also buried in St Edmunds. Edward's last wife was Mary Howard, daughter of Lord Howard of Effingham. She was eventually buried in St Margaret's, Westminster [197].

In 1568 Mary, Queen of Scots, was imprisoned by Queen Elizabeth after Mary's escape from Scotland [198]. Edward was suspected of being involved in a plot in 1571 to free the Scottish Queen from her confinement at Chatsworth House, Derbyshire. The suspicions were based on the fact that the main instigators of the plot were Edward's brother-in-laws the Stanleys, but nothing was proven. Queen Elizabeth did various progresses during her reign, and in 1575 she decided to visit Dudley Castle. It is not certain why she did this, given the general suspicion of Edward's allegiances, though perhaps it was to give him a clear picture of where they ought to have lain!

According to a letter dated 7th August 1575, she was due at Dudley on the 20th, but her visit was brought forward to the 12th.. Lord Burghley, then at Buxton, wrote to Secretary Francis Walsingham:

'I see the Queen's majestie is to be at Dudley on the 20th wher I am very sory, I can not be, specially for the satisfaction of my lord and lady Dudley, who I know would gladly have me there, the rather to further their sute, which otherwise I shall be most willing to do. and thynk it a very good deed.' [199]

The 'suit' Burleigh is referring to is likely to be the cessation of the annual rent of £12.5s.8d for part of Edward's lands.

Another letter from Walsingham explained why the Queen was going to Dudley earlier than she intended.

'Your lordship may perceive howe her majesty's determination to go to Worcester is altered; uppon advertisement from thence that the towne should be vystyted by small-pockes. This alteration as I suppose, dothe hasten her majesties repaire to Dudley Castell sooner than was determyned.'

The visit was a grand affair, local parishes sent supplies up to the castle. According to the Halesowen Churchwardens Accounts they sent:

'trayne and candles when the quene was at Dudley.' [200]

Figure 35: Portrait of Queen Elizabeth I. Queen Elizabeth came to stay at Dudley Castle in 1575. National Portrait Gallery, London.

The Queen stayed at John Giffard's house at Chillington on Thursday August 11th, and then travelled down to Dudley where she was 'wined and dined' in the castle. She may have stayed a whole day at Dudley, possibly taken up by hunting (her favourite sport), but carried on down to the Bishop's Palace at Hartlebury on Saturday 13th. As she did go to Worcester, presumably, the epidemic had receded. Edward was certainly there from the 14th to the 19th during the period of her visit to the city [201].

Queen Elizabeth allowed Edward to keep his rent in 1559. It did not die, however, because Edward gave it to his daughter Ann on her marriage to Francis Throckmorton. It was still held by their son John, but had reverted to the Crown by 1650.

Edward seems to have hit the recurring Sutton problem in 1579 - the inability to keep the estate solvent! A mortgage was granted to him on 21st July of that year. The deforcients were - William Cecil (Burleigh), Robert Dudley (Leicester), Walter Myldmay and Edward himself. The plaintiffs were Richard Crompton and James Kenryke. As nothing is heard of them again, presumably they were paid back. But in the late summer Cecil and Myldmay held the castle and lands. They granted its rents of 200 marks and 120 marks payable yearly, beginning the 24th November 1579 to Edward. These two grants related to the rented and knight's fees of the castle and land [202].

In 1582 another two estates transactions occurred, as part of the marriage settlement of Edward's 14 year old son to Theodosia Harrington. The new plaintiffs were Gilbert Gerrard, John Popham and Edward Harrington (Theodosia's father?). Edward received two sums of money, £2,720 and £4,000. Gerrard, Popham and Harrington held the estate for Edward's life and then it reverted to Lady Harrington and her husband's heirs. Edward paid a fine and he was allowed to retain his interest in the lands for the rest of this life. Edward was called on to pay £17.5s.0d. as part of a National Subsidy in 1584. It is likely that as he did not consider he owned the estate, he did not pay the subsidy. He is recorded as living at Himley and staying in Warwick in 1585, but Dudley Castle seems to have been virtually abandoned.

In January 1585 Mary, Queen of Scots, after numerous plots to free her, was moved back to Tutbury Castle. Her new jailer was the pedantic and officious Sir Amyas Paulet. Paulet's orders from Sir Francis Walsingham were that her imprisonment was to be transferred into the strictest possible confinement. Mary hated Tutbury, and by the end of the summer was unwell. Protest from the French Court (Mary had been married to a French king), to Queen Elizabeth led to Walsingham looking for an alternative accommodation. Paulet inspected a number of places and finally decided upon Chartley. Its owner, the Earl of Essex, objected, so Paulet was sent out to inspect other buildings, including Dudley Castle.

After his visit to Dudley, Sir Amyas wrote a letter to Sir Francis Walsingham showing his considerations.

'Sir - I would not faile, according to your former directions, to use all diligence for the removing of this Q. to Chartley, and to that purpose have caused great store of woodd to be felled; seal coal and charke coale to be

burned, tymber to be sawed; bere to be brewed, brick to be carried, and manie other like necessaries to be provided; but your letter of the iiiith of this present coming to my hands the viith of the same at ten of the clock at night, I retired my servants from Chartley, I discharged my carpenters and masons for one week, I disapointed as manie carriages as I could upon so short waminge, and stayed all my other proceedings there untill my return from Dudley castle, wher finding my L. Dudley absent I was forced to take my lodgings in one of the poorest townes that I have sene in my life,' and the next day tooke a full view of the castle, with the assent of my sayde L. who being then in Warwick, sent the keys with all expedition. The lodgings of this castle are not so many in number as I would so wish, and are also verie little and straight, saving the lodgings which must serve this Q. wch are so faire and commodious as she cannot desire to have them amended Touchinge the rest of the howse. these defects and inconveniences following cannot be denied: There is a great plenty of sea-coale, charck coale and fire woodd at hand; which cannot be had by for readie money, and therefore will prove chargeable when it shall be compared with the charge in other place, where fire woodd and coal came out of the Queenes owne woodd; and cost nothing but the makinge. Also the howse is utterly destitute of table boord; cup boords, fowrmes, stooles and bedsteades, saving that the hall and greate chamber are provided of table boord; the furnishing of which said wants prove to be a matter of great charge, which is not to be greatelie accounted of, if it be intended that this household shall remain there any tyme. A barn must be converted to a stable for the Governors horses, a matter of no great charge. This Queenes gentlemen servants will not like with their straight lodgings, because they have no inner chambers. The brewing vessels are somewhat decayed; and some are wanting, which may be supplied from Burton. The water far the kitchens and household must befett out of the dikes without the gate, and yet same will say that the pump wch standith in the myddest of the court yf yt were clensed would furnishe sufficient and good water, but I find others that doubt thereof. The chamber windows of this Q. lodgings are open upon the park, as likewise the windows of her kitchen, which I trust may be supplied by a good watch and a deep ditche, but speiclie by this Q. infirmitie which will not permit her to run away on her feet. These defect are recampensed yn parte with the strength of the howse in other respects, and with monie other good commodities. The counties of Worcester and Warwick adjoining yielding good plentie of all kinds of victuals, and at reasonable prices, saving that corne groweth to be deere in all these parts.

Thus, I have delivered unto you my simple opinion herein without partiality, referrring the same to your better consideration, and so do forbear to trouble you with anything ells until I shall hear from you what will be resolved.'

Mary was eventually moved to Chartley on Christmas Eve 1585. Walsingham worked very hard to get her convicted of treason, and she was eventually beheaded on 8th February 1587. Edward Sutton died in London in August 1586, and was buried in the 'family' vault in the church of St Margaret's Westminster on the 12th August. In his will he bequeathed his iron works, iron ore and woods to his wife Mary, Charles Howard (Lord Admiral), Henry Carye (Lord Chamberlain) and Sir John Littleton for a period of 21 years for the payment of his debts. He left £200 to his daughter Ann Throckmorton (now married to a Thomas Wilmer) and in a telling comment charged and commanded upon:

Figure 36: Dudley Plate found during the 1980's archaeological excavation.

'Edward; my oldeste sonne, that he doe noe manner of waye moleste or trouble the due performance of this may laste wyll and testament.' [203]

Edward Sutton III, 1586-1643: 25th Baron of Dudley

Edward was born in September 1567 and baptised on September 22nd, son of Edward II and Jane Stanley. He was educated at Lincoln's College, Oxford and matriculated on 24th July 1580. He inherited the Barony on his father's death in 1586. Edward's first problem as Lord Dudley was that the castle and park had reverted to Sir John Littleton as agreed in 1554. Like his father, he had signed an agreement to pay Littleton the £80 rent and the lands were returned to him. It looks as if Edward stopped paying these when Sir John died, and this led to some ill feeling between the Sutton's and the Littleton's.

Edward was stated to have joined the Naval action against the Spanish Armada in 1588, though no details have survived. As his step-grandfather was Lord Howard of Effingham, the Queen's Admiral, he was no doubt in the right position to join the Queen's ships if he had so wished. There is a record of him being made a Knight-of- the-Garter in 1590.

If Edward's father had financial problems, they were nothing compared with his son. The difference between the two was that Edward II never re-sorted to illegal or doubtful practices. There are three good examples of how Edward behaved in matters of finance.

Edward versus Thomas and Ann Wilmore

At some unknown date Edward II mortgaged the rents of his estate to his brother-in-law, Sir Edward Stanley. These were to revert on Stanley's death to Ann Wilmore (nee Sutton), Edward's sister. Edward III attempted to ignore this fact, and retained the rents for himself. In 1591 a special commission was held at Dudley Castle. Its purpose was in order to inquire into the payment of debts and annuities to Thomas Wilmore and Ann. The commission ordered Edward's bailiffs to pay Thomas and Ann out of the Baronies' profits. Edward ordered one of his bailiff's to confiscate the stock of a tenant in the interim in order to pay part to Thomas and Ann and part to pay Queen Elizabeth £17.15s.0d for a subsidy that he owed here. The unhappy bailiff was then sued by the tenant farmer!

In 1592 another commission ordered Edward to pay £206.13s.4d. or face sequestration (his property taken off him). Whether Edward tried to pay and failed, or did not bother trying, is not recorded, but in 1631 an order was made for the sequestration of his estate. All rents were to be paid directly to Thomas

Wilmore, who, after taking out sums to cover arrears and annuities, would give the residue to Edward [204].

Edward versus Martha Grosvenor

In 1585 Edward II leased Old Park to Richard Grosvenor for £1,000 and a yearly rent of £10. The agreement was that the contract would last for three lives, Richard himself, his wife Martha and his son Walter. When Edward III took over his father's property, Richard paid a heriot of £100 to keep the transaction legal, as was normal practice. Both Richard and his son died, but Martha continued the practice of paying the rent. The Grosvenors were Roman Catholic, an expensive religion after 1581, when all recusants were obliged to pay a tax of £20 a month. Martha's income began to suffer, and after her husband's death she made a secret agreement with Edward III that he was to use the facilities of the Park and pay her a rent. Edward took the park, but failed to pay the rent.

In the 1590's she took her case to Chancery. After a period of deliberation the Court told her in 1597 that it was not in their brief to make judgements on her kind of situation [205]. She then took the case to the Attorney General who ordered Edward to pay the monies owing since the 'Secret Agreement' was made. In 1617 Edward replied to the Attorney General that as the park was not his father's property when he leased it, the contract with the Grosvenors was null and void (this was possibly the Stanley mortgage). The Attorney General ordered if that were the case all monies paid by the Grosvenor's minus the yearly rents should be paid back to Martha. This was ignored, but a further litigation in 1620 led Ferdinando, Edward's only legitimate son, to agree to pay Martha £1,200. He paid £50 in 1621, the year of his death and Martha apparently received no more [206].

Edward versus Gilbert Littleton

Some time in Edward II's lifetime he had sold his interests in Prestwood and Ashwood to Sir John Littleton. This was inherited by John's son Gilbert. In 1592 Edward III decided to claim it back again by saying his father had no right to sell something that did not belong to him (his lands being mortgaged). Presumably Gilbert had no intention of accepting this, and kept the lands. Rather than go to court, Edward decided to take the law into his own hands. On the night of the 12th October, Edward led a band of 130 retainers into the woods and stole *'fourteen kyne, one bull and eight fat oxen'*. The animals were at first driven into the bailey of Dudley Castle, and then Edward decided to send them to Coventry market. It looks as if he had second thoughts about this, and he sent more retainers to bring them back to the castle, just in case any of Gilbert's men attempted to rescue them. The cattle were eventually slaughtered in Dudley Castle. Gilbert exhibited a bill in the Court of the Star Chamber for this offence and others. One of the others was that Edward had '*suffered his father's old servant Thomas Homes to die in Worcester Gaol for his Lordship's debts.*' [207]

Apart from these less endearing traits Edward also practiced his father's technique of acquiring ready money by mortgaging parts of his estate. This occurred virtually every year between 1595 and 1609. The sums varied with which estate he was using as security for the loan. They included:-

1596 £300
1597 £1,300
1598 £700+£100+£400
1601 £120
1603 £2,400
1609 £100

Edward also leased various parts of his estates. The Levesons of Wolverhampton added a large part of Sedgley to their holdings of Dudley land in 1609 with Sir Walter Leveson's lease.

Edward was summoned to Parliament in London in 1595 and attended them quiet regularly until 1639; perhaps while he was there was one of the rare occasions he saw his wife. Although he had married Theodosia Harrington, there was little love there, and she does not appear to have lived at Dudley Castle. Though they did have a son called Ferdinando, born on the 4th September 1588, by the late 1590's she had left him. In the 1620's she is recorded as selling some of her jewellery. The historian Twamley thought she was parting with her possessions due to her husband's neglect. It is much more likely that she was financially in a better position than her husband. She was certainly living in the Royal Court in the 1630's, and in London in the 1640's, so she could not have been that short of resources. Edward meanwhile took a mistress, a local woman called Elizabeth Tomlinson, by whom he had eleven children, Dud Dudley the iron master being one of them [208].

Edward continued to part with his lands. In 1612 he is granting reversion and remainders of his lands fee tail to a George Baggley. Sir William Cockayne also held large elements of Edward's lands. Then in 1622 a London jeweller called William Ward began to pick up Edward's mortgages. A substantial part of the estate was mortgaged to him by 1628. Edward received £20,000 for it. Ward had more on his mind than land however. As an extremely wealthy man, he now wanted status, and by tying himself to the Sutton family he could gain it. An agreement was made that Ward's son, called Humble, should marry Edward's only legitimate granddaughter (Ferdinando's daughter), Frances [209].

Edward probably had little time to spend his new windfall, as his whole estate (but the castle) was sequestered in 1631 to Thomas and Ann Wilmer. An agreement that Edward should reside in the castle and concerning its repair, dated July 1635, suggests it had passed to Ward by this time. Ward spent most of the 1630's acquiring other parts of the old estate. Finding out who held what and for how long must have been a mammoth task considering the Sutton's financial habits.

By 1639 most of Edward's debts had been paid off, but he was left with a very limited income. King Charles I called him to join his expedition against the Scottish Covenanters in 1639. His financial state is best described in his own words:

'Though I have passed over my estate to Mr Warde, who married my grandchild for the payment of debts and their present maintenance, yet if I can either horse or foot it I will attend; though unable to serve his majesty according to my desires and in such sort as is required.'

As by this time he was 73, one would have thought that he was also a little old for fighting, even if he could have afforded it! On the outbreak of the Civil War in 1641, Edward armed the castle for the coming fray, but he died on 23rd June 1643, and was buried in St Edmunds Church, Dudley.

6. Civil War and Dudley Castle

On the 22nd August 1642 King Charles I raised the Royal Standard at Nottingham, and the Civil War had started. Virtually immediately Edward III formed a Fund Raising Committee to support the king in the surrounding counties to his castle [210]. In September of the same year, a Parliamentary broadsheet printed in London reported that Dudley Castle had been taken over *'by some gentlemen', 'and there is many Collyers and Naylers are come in to them, and day and night they beat their Drums, and shoote off their Musquets, to the terrour of the Country; they have taken some Iron-workes of Master Folies, where it is said they are casting of Ordnance, and making Iron Bullets : And it is said there are 400.'* [211]. It is more than likely that Edward Sutton had called some of these local 'men-to-arms' in support of the king. Whether this was the type of men he wanted is a moot point, but at least to begin with Dudley Castle had shown which side it was going to support.

In the same month John Beaumont of Wednesbury and a force of 400 Welsh recruits and a regiment of Staffordshire infantry arrived in Dudley [212]. It was likely that Edward decided that John Beaumont did not have the experience to take over the garrison as he chose an ardent local Royalist, Sir Thomas Leveson from Wolverhampton, as Governor of the Castle's garrison. Leveson was a Roman Catholic and had originally left England, as he was not allowed to bear arms. He had been on the continent fighting, but on hearing about the coming war had come home straight into the Dudley job. He stated in a later letter dated February 1643 that on his arrival at Dudley they had plenty of volunteers, but not the right sort, besides which they did not have any arms, and was not able to purchase any. He stated that many of them had been dismissed before he had arrived, which was a pity, as the Royalist cause needed all the support it could get [213].

The Dudley folk probably had mixed feelings about having so many soldiers garrisoned close to the town. On the one side there was nowhere else for them to spend money but in the inns and taverns of the town, and no doubt they bought other things from the traders. The downside of course is that men who did as they were told all day, rescinded responsibility when they went out for a drink at night, and drunkenness, fights and destruction of property were three of the hazards that they had to put up with. Another was paying for it all. The earliest reference to taxes was in July 1643, when Colonel Leveson levied taxes for the support of the garrison in Seisdon Hundred, Staffordshire and in Warwickshire close to the Castle. Monthly contributions included: money, provisions, wood and *'Seaven score bedds'*. His tax collecting continued into 1644 [214]. In the August people as far away as Hatherton are recorded as paying £1 for *'Dudley Castell'*. [215]

Colonel Leveson was a professional soldier, and garrison work was not to his liking, so any opportunity he had to get out of the castle he took. His earliest recorded raid was on Chillington House. It had been taken in the August by Sir William Brereton for Parliament, but Leveson re-took it in the early September. The house had undergone a great deal of damage, and it was unsuitable to be re-garrisoned [216]. On the 18th December 1643 he had a request from Sir Thomas Holte of Aston Hall near Birmingham to place 40 musketeers from Dudley Castle in the Hall. It was not before time, as a Parliamentary force of 1,200 men quickly besieged the hall. The odds were against the defenders, and after continuous bombardment they surrendered on the 28th December [217]. (The shattered balustrade of the staircase can still be seen today in the Hall.)

Meanwhile Leveson himself, with Captain Heaveningham, led a force on the 21st December to take Lapley House from the Parliamentarian troops that held it. Heaveningham was particularly bold in the attack, as he climbed a wall, ran across a courtyard and put a ladder up to a window and climbed in - all under fire! They were successful, and left a small garrison there to guard it. An attempt was made to retake it by troops from Stafford, but they were routed by the Dudley defenders [218].

On the 4th January 1644 King Charles promoted Leveson to be High Sheriff of Staffordshire, but Leveson's arguments with his superior Lord Loughborough increased, and the king reprimanded him for it. Presumably he was forgiven in May, as he was made Colonel and told to *'impress, raise, enroll and retayne one regiment of fifteen hundred foote'*. Meanwhile the national status of the war had brought Prince Rupert into the West Midlands, and on 24th April 1644 Colonel Leveson ordered the Constable of Wrottesley to supply him with foodstuffs to be stored at Dudley Castle and to be picked up by the Prince [219]. On the 13th May 1644 Colonel Leveson again ordered the Constable of Wrottesley to supply 37 men furnished with *'mattocks, crowes of iron, baskets, and such like tooles, for fortification,'* to be brought to the castle the following day. This was due to his hearing that Lord Denbigh was about to invest the castle. No force arrived, so Leveson took the main part of the garrison to join Prince Rupert's army, which now proceeded north to rescue Lancashire and Yorkshire from the Parliamentary clutches [220]. This left Dudley Castle with a skeleton garrison commanded by Lieutenant-Colonel Beaumont.

The First Siege of Dudley: 1644

In June of 1644 Lord Denbigh led a 3,500 strong Parliamentary force against Dudley Castle and laid siege to it. Despite the fact that he only had one effective cannon, a weapon called the 'Stafford Great Piece' (a 32lb demi-cannon that had served as a whipping post in Stafford Market Place), he bombarded the castle with it, inflicting some damage on the keep [221]. Local tradition has it that the cannon was mounted on Kates Hill, directly opposite the southern side of the Keep. A cannon ball was found underneath the floor during an excavation in the 1980's. It must have entered one of the windows in the keep, ricocheted around the walls and then buried itself under the plaster of the floor. All Beaumont could do was keep his head down, and hope his few

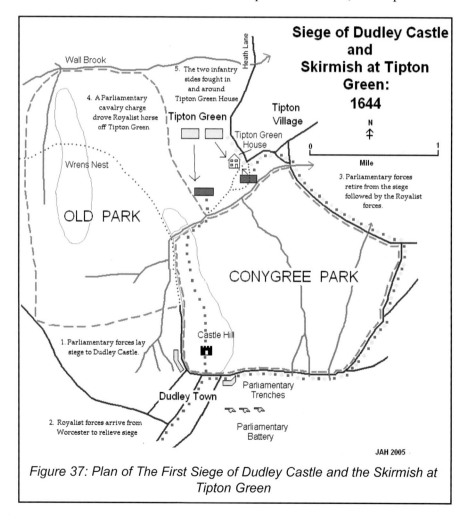

Figure 37: Plan of The First Siege of Dudley Castle and the Skirmish at Tipton Green

Figure 38: Cannon balls & shot excavated in the castle. Source: DUCAP.

men could repulse a general attack. The king was at Worcester at the time, and when he heard about the siege sent Lord Wilmot, with 4,000 horse and foot, to relieve it.

Denbigh's scouts had reported that the Royalists were getting close to Dudley on the 10th June, and he prepared to withdraw his forces to Walsall on the 11th. The Royalist forces moved far more rapidly than he envisaged, and arrived on the morning of the 11th, which meant that the Parliamentarians had to beat a hasty retreat. There are two reports about this battle, one from the Royalists and the other from the Parliamentarians, and apart from the names, one would wonder if they were talking about the same event. If you mix and match the descriptions there is a chance of working out what happened. The Royalists reported that Lord Wilmot charged the Parliamentary forces and ran right through them, and then stated that Lord Denbigh was not advised to 'leave his trenches' to come to their rescue. As he would not have had time to dig trenches on Tipton Green, this must have been an action in front of Dudley Castle before Denbigh had moved off to Tipton Green [222].

Whatever happened, the Royalists must have given Denbigh the time to retire, and his forces chose to go east of Castle Hill on the Dudley-Wednesbury road. By the time they got to Tipton, the Royalists were again nearly on them. In those days the lanes that ran though cultivated land were narrow, and it was not until Denbigh reached the common that was Tipton Green that he had any chance of defending himself. Just as he reached it, Lieutenant-Colonel Beaumont, who was aware what was going on, took a cavalry force out of the castle and rode along the top of Castle Hill towards Tipton Green. With Royalist's to his side and Royalists at his back Denbigh had no choice but to fight.

Lord Denbigh reported the event in a letter to Parliament, stating that the password of the day was WORCESTER for the Royalists and GOD, KING AND PARLIAMENT for the Parliamentarians. The skirmish began at about 2 o'clock in the afternoon and finished about five. He ordered Sir Thomas Middleton to take his regiments of horse and foot and prepare to defend the Green. There was a mansion on the Green, the home of a Mr Edward Dudley, kinsman to the Barons of Dudley, and Middleton sent musketeers to take it.

The fight started on the west flank when Major Fraser, who commanded Denbigh's Regiment of Horse, allowed Beaumont's cavalry and the main Royalist Horse to come on to the Green. He led a charge that broke the Royalists lines and then routed them. He pursued them as far as the bottom of Castle Hill inflicting losses. According to Denbigh, over 1,500 Royalist horse were engaged in the conflict, and he estimated that they lost 60-100 men. The Parliamentarian losses were less, only 10 men.

Meanwhile on the east flank the fighting went on around the mansion. The heroes of the hour were the Staffordshire Regiment, led by Colonel Symon Rugeley and Major Pinkeney. They defended the house for nearly two hours, but eventually the Royalists retired. The losses here were surprisingly slight, the Royalists losing only 16 men; what condition the mansion was after was not stated! Denbigh held the field for a further two hours, but the Royalists were not going to fight, so he retired to Walsall. A letter sent from the Castle was captured by the Parliamentarians the day after the fight. It stated:

To the chief Mufician in Dudley Caftle

Thefe are to will and require you to bring all your inftruments of Muficke, efpeciall your loud Mufic to his Majefties Caftle at Dudley. If any of you fhall fail, I will not fail to fire his or their houfes for their difrepects. From his Majesties Caftle at Dudley.

T. Beamont.

It appeared that Lieutenant-Colonel Beaumont intended to celebrate the lifting of the siege with a party! The damage done to the castle had to be repaired, and on the 22nd of June another order went out to the Constable of

Wrottesley, to supply men or to pay men 12d a day to repair the damage that had been inflicted on the castle during the siege. An additional instruction on the 23rd was an order *'to carry lime, coales, wood, timber, stone and hay' to the castle'*. [223]

By late June Sir William Brereton advanced on Wolverhampton. The Dudley forces were in no position to stop this happening, so Leveson's home town and his own semi-fortified hall had to be abandoned. The king sent a letter to the Staffordshire landowners saying that as Dudley was the last bastion of royal power in the county, they should feel obliged to give any assistance that Colonel Leveson requested [224]. Leveson, however, had his own problems at the time. The Dudley Castle forces were still with Prince Rupert's army. The Prince met a large Parliamentary army at Marston Moor near York on the 2nd July, and was defeated in battle. Leveson and what was left of his men returned to Dudley [225].

In October the Parliamentarian 'Tinker' Fox, who was garrisoned in Edgbaston House, was thought to be becoming a nuisance, so forces from Dudley Castle and Worcester were sent to flush him out. Fox by name and fox by nature, the Tinker managed to repel the raid [226].

Sir Thomas Leveson was at Dudley Castle in December, as he wrote a letter there to the king. It is a little obtuse, but it probably related to the Siege of Lichfield. By the following year the garrison began to raid again more successfully. Sergeant-Major Heaveningham was sent on the 1st February 1645 with a party of 400 foot and horse to successfully plunder Birmingham [227].

In May the king was on the move again, and most of the garrison of Dudley Castle attended him at Cofton Hall on the 15th of that month. King Charles I intended to inflict a crushing defeat on the Parliamentarians, and was picking up soldiers for this battle. Colonel Leveson and his men joined the Royal army. They moved up to Leicester, which they took with a great deal of loss of both civilian and military life, before moving on to Naseby on the 14th June. At this, the last major battle of the civil war, the king suffered a definitive defeat [228].

After the Battle of Naseby, all must have realised it was the beginning of the end for the Royalist cause. The fact that payment of service became a common problem can be seen. Leveson wrote a letter to the king in the January of 1646. In it he explained it was not good policy to cut his soldiers' arrears, and that many of them are thinking of giving up the fight [229]. The King could do little about it, however, as parliament held the purse strings.

Sir William Brereton began to take the Royalist garrisons one by one in the west midlands. On 6th April Captain Tuthill, one of Brereton's officers, intercepted a letter sent from Dudley Castle, intended to go to the Royalist Lichfield garrison. The letter had been written by Leveson, and he wrote that he had had news from Worcester that the Scots Army was to support the King, and was marching to Newark. He felt that this factor might induce the Parliamentary forces to make an extra push against the Royalist garrisons, and so all should be on their guard [230].

Brereton attended the surrender of Tutbury Castle on Tuesday 21st April, but his letters show that his prime objective was still Lichfield. As late as 30th April he was considering ordering a mortar that had been used at Belvoir to aid in the taking of Lichfield Close. Lichfield was a hard nut to crack however, and Brereton next turned his sights on Dudley Castle. A document dated 4th May, made as far away as Uttoxeter, was for the inhabitants to provided £16 for bread, beer, cheese and drink for Leek soldiers marching against Dudley - Brereton was on his way! [231].

The Last Siege of Dudley Castle: 1646

The first document in Brereton's Letter Book that related to Dudley was on Friday 23rd April. This was a report on the state of the Castle made by Captain Seale, a Parliamentary officer. The Royalist garrison was in complete control of the Dudley area at the time, and therefore Seale appears to have been acting as an intelligence officer. He reported that the Castle was garrisoned by 265 foot and horse soldiers - the horse in the minority (on the surrender, Brereton reported that 340 foot and horse marched out). Seale also gave a run-down on the situation of the Castle, and played down what Brereton later stated was a virtually impregnable stronghold. He knew enough about the Castle, however, to recommend that 'the Mount' (the area between the Lower and Triple Gateways) had to be taken first. He also suggested, correctly, that the 'new buildings' (the 16th century rebuilding of the Great Hall complex) was mineable. He implied in his report that a previous Parliamentary barrage had damaged the Barnt Tower [Keep], possibly choking the well inside. Excavation has not disclosed a well in the centre of the Keep, but it is not impossible that one may exist within one of the southern drum towers.

Saturday 24th April: As part of Brereton's preparations for the siege of Dudley, he ordered troopers to come up from their garrisons at Leicester, Stafford and Tamworth. Amongst the officers mentioned were Captain Ffradshaw from Tamworth and Captain Tuthill from Stafford. That evening an engagement of some kind occurred in the Enville/Kinver area, the result of which was that Royalist Ensign Capelwood and some of his men were cap-

Figure 39: Drawing of the last siege. Source: David Stevens.

tured and taken to Wrottesley (4 miles due west of Wolverhampton), where they were imprisoned. Parliamentary soldiers - Dickin, Worsley, Rottley, Lane and Mytton - also involved in the engagement were taken and incarcerated in Dudley Castle.

Sunday 25th April: To judge by what Brereton found when he arrived on the Tuesday, Colonel Leveson knew that Dudley was next on his list, and had sent some of his soldiers out on a foraging raid. It is probable that this had already started by the weekend.

Monday 26th April: Brereton left Lichfield to march on Dudley with the Leicestershire, Staffordshire and Shropshire Foot and Horse. They reached Walsall by nightfall, but a guard of horse was sent on to Dudley to keep an eye on the Royalists. Probably due to the fact that they were late with their pay, the Shropshires began to get somewhat disruptive.

Tuesday 21st April: The grumbling about pay had developed into a full scale mutiny by the morning, so Brereton had to leave the Shropshire Foot behind. They did follow up the main force, but the march degenerated into a 'pub crawl', and at Wednesbury some drunken soldiers killed a young man for failing to tell them where the next tavern was. Brereton meanwhile arrived at Dudley at 11 o'clock. The Royalist troops were still in the town, driving cattle through to the Castle, which suggests that Brereton's Horse, who had arrived the evening before, had been ordered only to observe.

On the entrance of the Parliamentary soldiers, Leveson proceeded to order his own men to start setting houses in the town on fire. Whether this was to cover the withdrawal, or part of his plan to clear the buildings close to the Castle, is not clear. Leveson had already pulled down the Church of St Edmunds for strategic purposes, sometime between January and this date. Five houses were set on fire, and these and a number of others were completely destroyed. Parliamentary soldiers were ordered to put the fire out. To the soldiers' astonishment, the townsmen of Dudley failed to assist in the fire fighting. But as the Royalists in the castle were firing down into the town this is understandable. It must have been pandemonium at this time, as Leveson's men had left *'manie hundreds of cattle'* milling around in the market place. The noise and the flames would have terrified them. Brereton ordered that these were to be quietened down and returned to their owners.

Figure 40: Drawing of Siege of Dudley Castle, Source.
DMBC Ludlow/Boland

Figure 41: Pottery Grenade. Source: DUCAP.

With the Royalists now bottled up in the Castle, it was Brereton's plan to keep them there. He ordered his *'pyoneers'* to start constructing a wall using the stone of the demolished Church of St Edmunds. The wall ran from the site of the Church to the Priory - in the vicinity of what would later be called The Broadway. The *'brestworke'* was built, according to Brereton, because most of the ground was limestone, which prohibited trenching. It seems likely that with everything now organised, Brereton set off to Birmingham to pick up some money for his men's wages. Meanwhile, unknown to Brereton or any other Parliamentary soldier, King Charles, who decided his English forces were incapable of reviving, had left Oxford some time in the day, with the intention of joining the Scots Army at Newark.

Wednesday 28th April: During the morning the three companies of the Shropshire Foot who had mutinied turned up, and were sent over to the Priory to act as the garrison. They seem to have returned to their duties with great reluctance and in a very half-hearted manner. Within a very short time they were *'straggling abroad'* and *'fishing'* in the Priory ponds. The sentries who had been set were sleeping on duty (no doubt sleeping off the previous day's drinking session!). It looks as if none of them had any intention of working, as the musketeers, who normally had their matches alight on duty, were also not prepared for what was to happen next!

Leveson's sentries in the Castle were within a half musket shot of the Priory, and no doubt observed this spectacle with great amusement. It was an opportunity they could not fail to miss. A company of soldiers attacked immediately, and within a short time they had killed two of the Shropshires and captured the Priory with its arms and supplies. Not all Brereton's soldiers were so unprofessional however, and Colonel Hackes (Governor of Leicester) with the Leicestershire Horse and his Troop and Cornet Paget, with another guard, charged to the rescue. The Royalists could not hold the Priory, and retreated back up the hill into the Castle, no doubt leaving a very crestfallen group of Shropshire soldiers behind them.

Meanwhile, up in the Castle they were experiencing their own problems. Some time on the Tuesday or Wednesday morning, Lieutenant-Colonel John Beaumont's wife had died. Dorothy Beaumont could not have been a particularly old woman, as she had given birth to a child in the Castle (which had died the same day), in the September of 1644. What caused her death is unknown. Leveson now sounded his drum for someone in the Parliamentary Army to come and parley, so that he could arrange her burial in the Upper Church of St Thomas. At least two soldiers climbed the steep path up from the High Street to the Elizabethan Gateway to receive the message. The soldiers on guard, either due to nervousness (the Priory action?) or because they were trigger happy, shot them dead!

A message did get through however, but was received by Captain Ffradshaw, the officer whose men had been shot, and he was not at all sympathetic, as his letter in reply showed. The message eventually reached the officer-in-command in Brereton's absence - Adjutant General James Louthiane. Louthiane explained that Sir William Brereton was away and sent a pass for twelve people - not including the deceased's husband - to attend the funeral at St. Thomas'.

Brereton's business in Birmingham with Sir Richard Skiffington, Colonel Willoughby (Governor of Coventry) and the Coventry Committee, concluded with the arrangement of funds, levied from Warwickshire to pay the Besiegers (Leaguers), to be forwarded to Dudley through an agent. By the end of the day, Brereton had returned from Birmingham and wrote to Colonel Leveson, confirming the arrangements for the funeral but condemning the Governor's action of firing the town and killing his soldiers under a flag of truce. Leveson immediately replied, thanking Brereton for his '*civilitie*' in allowing the burial and apologising for the two soldiers being shot, which he stated was '*contrary to my orders*'. He pointed out that as far as firing the town was concerned, his duty as a soldier was to always prevent the enemy from being in a situation of '*advantage*', and felt that the General would no doubt have acted in a similar way if he had been placed in the same circumstances.

While in Birmingham, Brereton had received a petition from the townsmen requesting that he make overtures to Colonel Leveson to free Edward Ensor, one of their number who was imprisoned by the Royalists in Dudley Castle. In his letter to Leveson, Brereton said that if Ensor was released he would return the favour. Colonel Leveson released Ensor to Brereton, and stated that he had three others, Howell, Braye and Carew, whom he would release in exchange for Capelwood at Wrottesley.

Figure 42: The Carew ring found in excavation in 1980's, DUCAP.

A letter from Lady Frances Ward to Brereton is an interesting example of the Dudley family's involvement in the Civil War in the area. Lady Dudley had apparently been called to Oxford but still expected her affairs in Dudley to be carried out. She referred to Major Christopher Heaveningham of the Dudley Garrison on a previous commission, as having been given only a limited pass to see her in Oxford, and requested that he be given another pass.

She finished her letter with a peculiar comment for a loyal Royalist, for she wrote that if Heaveningham was sent to her Brereton *'you shall recive an answer attending to your expectacon'*. The most obvious reading of this comment is that Lady Dudley, who must have known of the King's departure on the preceding day, was intimating this knowledge. A ten day pass was issued to Mr. Edward Asehurst of Black Parke on the same day, but it is not known if he was Lady Frances's messenger.

Thursday 29th April: By Thursday the two sides seemed to have settled down to what both may have considered was going to be a long siege. It does not appear that Brereton had any intention of risking the lives of his men by attempting to take the Castle by storm. A note in the papers referred to Edward Ensor's agreement to pay 27s. 6d. *'as marshall fees'*. It is possible that this was some kind of fee for his release. Brereton's main concern now was the prisoners issue. He wrote to Leveson firstly stating that he did not hold the Governor to blame for the two men being shot at the parley. He also stated that he knew nothing of the prisoners Leveson referred to in his communication. He pointed out that as far as Capelwood was concerned, he was due to be executed under the same rules that Leveson previously chose to adhere to when he executed two Parliamentary soldiers. He would, however, exchange Capelwood and the men captured with him for the Parliamentary soldiers held prisoner in Dudley Castle. Leveson's reply was that he was sending the prisoners he had referred to in his earlier letter, but was not able to return the men Brereton had requested.

Friday 30th April: Brereton wrote three reports relating to the events of 27th and 28th April, one went to *'The Committee of Both Kingdoms'*, one to the Speaker of the House of Commons and the last to Messrs Ashurst, Moris and Ashton.

He also wrote a reply to Leveson's letter from the previous day about the prisoners. He was far from happy about Leveson's arrangements, and demanded that he be sent the men he requested, and not those the Royalist Governor chose to give him. He asked specifically for a Richard Lure of Kinver, and said that Capelwood and company were on their way from Wrottesley. He added that he had no intention of doing business this way in the future.

[After April we have a problem with Brereton's days and dates - the only explanation of which is that he or his secretary considered that April had 29 rather than 30 days.]

Saturday to Tuesday, 1st to 5th May: Leveson requested permission sometime in this period to send messengers to the King at Oxford for instructions. Brereton allowed the messengers to go and return. What their instructions were, if there were any in the King's absence, is not known. The King himself had joined the Scots Army on 5th May. The Governor no doubt had no intention of giving away to Brereton that the King was not where Parliament thought he was.

Thursday [called Wednesday], 6th May: Brereton sent a Summons to Leveson requesting that the Castle be surrendered to the Parliamentary forces. He demanded that his Conditions of Surrender be accepted by 9 o'clock on Friday [called Thursday] morning.

Friday [called Thursday] 7th May: Leveson wrote to the Parliamentary camp requesting a pass to visit Oxford concerning the Summons. Brereton wrote back enclosing a pass for Beaumont and Heaveningham. Leveson asked if they could be allowed to go to the King. Brereton rightly guessed he was stalling for time and refused. Leveson now agreed to treat for the '*sessacon of hostilitie*', and a surrender was arranged on Brereton's conditions for the following Thursday, [called Wednesday].

Saturday [called Friday] 8th May: Brereton seems to have journeyed to Coventry, as a letter written to Sir Thomas Fairfax (Lord General of the Parliamentary Forces) was sent from there. Sir William congratulated Sir Thomas on the surrender of Banbury and the commencement of the siege of Oxford. Brereton implied in his letter that Fairfax had requested troopers from him, and apologised for his inability to supply them, due to his not having enough for the siege at Dudley.

Sunday to Monday [called Saturday/Sunday] 9th and 10th May: With Dudley on the verge of surrender, it seems likely that Brereton returned to Lichfield.

Tuesday [called Monday] 11th May: Brereton wrote from Lichfield to Mr. Lenthal, the Speaker of the House of Commons, reporting the events leading up to the surrender of Dudley Castle. He also wrote to Sir Thomas Fairfax about the surrender, reporting that it would take place on Wednesday, 13th May [13th was a Thursday].

Wednesday [called Tuesday] 12th May: Sir William Brereton rode back to Dudley.

Thursday [called Wednesday] 13th May: Colonel Thomas Leveson with 40 officers and 300 men marched out of the Castle, leaving a twelve months supply of provisions. Brereton officially took over at 1 o'clock and transferred Captain Tuthill, Governor of Rushall, to Dudley to form the Parliamentary garrison. His letter to Ashurst and Swinfen the same day recommended that as Dudley was such a strong Castle, it should not be destroyed, but preserved for the use of Parliament, and that the Counties of Worcestershire and Staffordshire should contribute to the charge of its upkeep.

John Tanner was instructed to account for all the arms left in the Castle by the Royalists. His report showed a lack of artillery - only two cannons and a few hand cannons were found. With plenty of powder, match and shot and 242 muskets and carbines, they were well equipped to defend the walls however. Tanner also suggested in his report that other arms may have been hidden about the Castle.

Wednesday 19th May: Brereton wrote a pass at Lichfield for Sir Henry Skipwith, Baronet, a member of the Dudley Castle garrison. The pass was attached to Dudley Castle Articles of Surrender.

It is difficult to say how much local support the garrison had. A letter sent from Richard Pershouse a week after the surrender suggested that at least the gentry supported the king, but they did not seem to like Thomas Leveson.

'...It is twelve dayes since I came home, this Hanson being the first carriar I could send by. Dudley is lately yeelded (on Tewsday last) to Sir Will. Breretoon. I being myselfe ther saw Collonell Leveson gallop away with manie thousand curses of the cuntrie people, whoe would certainly have kil'd him had hee not beene strongly guarded with 2 troops of horse of the Parliament whoe were assigned to him by the Articles for his convoy. Hee and Dibdale and certain others (his retinue) are gone for France to looke after his cash which hee sent thether; nowe our contrie is satisfied that hee servde the King a little, but himselfe most. The Castle was yeelded without any shot of the Parliament (having great store of ammunition and provision in it). I would be loath, for all his gaines, to depart with soe much disgrace as hee did. I beleeve our cuntrie wilbe shortly cleerde, then I hope you will be as good as your word. I hope for my composition; if I stay till Michaelmass it will be noe prejudice to mee, God send better times. I purpose to write to you again at Hanson's returne.' [232].

Thomas Leveson and Christopher Heaveningham both went abroad after they left Dudley. In a letter dated 12th September 1652 Colonel Thomas Leveson was said to have died four days before, after fifteen days of sickness. What happened to Christopher Heaveningham is still a mystery [233].

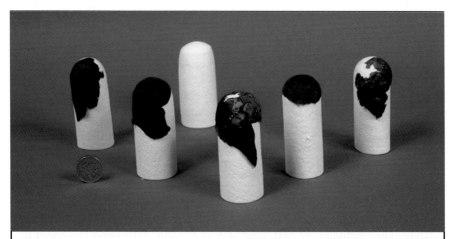

Figure 43: The World's oldest Condoms found in the garderobe (lavatory) of the keep at Dudley Castle during excavation in the 1980's. Some of the officers who were garrisoned in the castle had fought abroad before the English Civil War and these 'reusable' condoms are liable to have belonged to them. At this time they were used to prevent disease rather than pregnancy. Source. DUCAP/DMBC.

Frances Ward, 1635-1697: 26th Baron of Dudley

Frances was born at Dudley Castle on 23rd July 1611 and baptised there. She was the daughter of Ferdinando Sutton and Honora Seymour (daughter of Lord Beauchamp). Her mother died in 1620 and was buried in St Edmunds, and her father died in the following year of smallpox and was buried in St. Margaret's, London [234]. It seems likely that she was brought up by her grandfather, Edward III. When Edward's debts became insurmountable in 1628, he married her off to Humble Ward, the son of William Ward, a wealthy jeweller. Her husband acquired most of the rights of the estate, but not the barony. Frances herself was raised to Baroness Dudley in 1635. Humble bought the title Baron Birmingham off Charles I when the family were at Oxford.

Although Frances was technically a Royalist, her relations with the Parliamentary General, Sir William Brereton (a descendant of the Brereton who her great grandfather had served under in Ireland) was extremely cordial - so much so that it seems the family were friends before the war. Over a month before Brereton laid siege to Dudley Castle, a contract of marriage had been made between Frances' son Edward and Brereton's daughter Frances. Now the cryptic message may have been referring to that, but Frances must have known at the same time as she was writing that King Charles had left Oxford to join a Scottish Army. It failed, and Charles was captured and the war came to an end. Perhaps she was well aware of the situation, and the letter to Leveson was to surrender the castle, which he in fact did a fortnight later.

This may have been opportunism on Frances's part, when she saw the Royalist side was going to lose, but not necessarily so! She must have known Brereton's influence was limited regarding the sequestration of Royalist property, besides which, Frances Brereton's dowery was over £1,000. Sir William was paying a sizeable sum for his daughter to marry a potential Baron of Dudley - this on top of a war that personally must have cost him a fortune.

Six months after the Castles's surrender, the local Parliamentary Committee decided to sequester the estates of the Barony. Despite the fact that Brereton advised Parliament not to damage Dudley Castle, parts were demolished in 1647. This included the east, west and south side of the keep, the upper part and the Barbican of the Triple gateway, the Chapel, the Great Chamber and the west curtain wall, only the Renaissance Range was left. Living in a ruin was not to Frances and Humbles' liking. During the war they had been living at Wrens Nest House, as that is where several of their children were born, but on William Ward's death the family moved to Himley [235].

Parliament sold the Crown rent to Henry Sanders in 1650, though this reverted to the Crown in 1672. Getting the land back was a problem. In 1652 Humble Ward conveyed the Castle and his lands to Sir William Brereton and his sons, in the hope that this would free them from sequestration. It did not, and it was only by getting Oliver Cromwell to intervene in 1656 that the estates were returned. Frances died and was buried at Himley on 11th August 1697 [236].

7. The House of Ward and Lea

Figure 44: Ward Coat-of-Arms

Edward Ward I, 1697-1701: 27th Baron of Dudley

Edward Ward became Baron Ward of Birmingham when his father died in 1670 and he became Baron Dudley of Dudley Castle in 1697, when his mother died. He had married Francis Brereton, the daughter of Sir William, who had laid siege to the castle in 1646. His early children were born at Wrens Nest House in the 1650's, which suggests that this place was reserved for the eldest son to live in. After the death of his father he appeared to be living at Himley. In 1687 the Duke of Monmouth commissioned Edward as Deputy Lieutenant of Stafford [237]. Edward took his seat in the House of Lords in 1670 and 1697-8, and died in 1701 [238].

Edward Ward II, 1701-1704: 28th Baron of Dudley

All Edward's sons died before him, so it was his grandson, the offspring of his third son William Ward, who succeeded him. He was born in 1683 and married Diane Howard at St Margarets Westminster in 1703. He died in 1704 at Whitehall, London, of smallpox [239].

Edward Ward III, 1704-1731: 29th Baron of Dudley

Edward, born in 1704, was the only son of Edward II. He was made Deputy Lieutenant of Worcester in 1706. It was during his day that probably the last of the huge oak trees that had once clothed Pensnett Chase was cut down. It was made into a Long Table that was moved into the Great Hall, according to the Reverend Luke Booker of Dudley, who had met a lady who had attended the event [240].

The Wards were better businessmen than their predecessors, and the fact that the industrial revolution was about to take off led them to utilise the

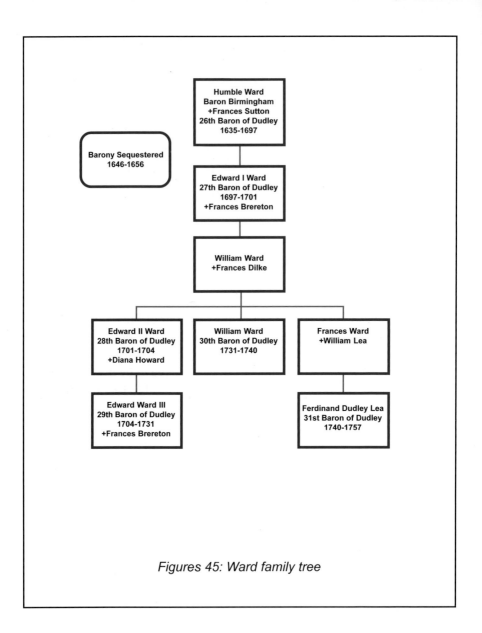

Figures 45: Ward family tree

112

minerals that lay beneath their grounds. They were also at the forefront of industrial technology, seen by the fact that the first example of Thomas Newcomen's Fire Engine (Steam Engine) was installed at Bloomfield Colliery, northeast of the Castle, in 1712. A sales brochure drawn up to sell it showed the castle in the background [241]. Edward died unmarried at Ashtead (his mothers home) in 1731 [242].

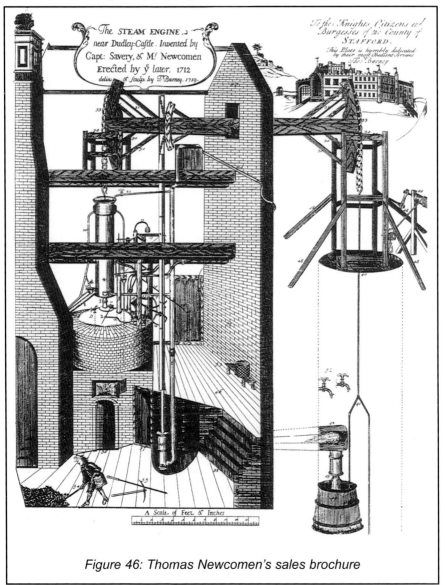

Figure 46: Thomas Newcomen's sales brochure

William Ward, 1731-1740: 30th Baron of Dudley

William was born in the 1680's, the younger brother of Edward II. He inherited the barony on his brother's death. It may have been in his time that a ball occurred in the castle that was written about by Mrs Sherwood. Mrs Sherwood was a writer of moral children's fiction. She was born in Worcestershire and lived in the City of Worcester from 1816 till 1849. In that period time she wrote most of her books. Dudley Castle was published in the Spring of 1832, and it concerned the sins of vanity, pride, envy and discontent. The story tells of a visit to the castle and lessons that can be learned from studying it, but the interesting point is that she tells the story of a servant who once had attended a ball at the castle. By examining the structure of the Sharrington range, it is too close to what the rooms would have looked like for it to be fully invented. Who Mrs Sherwood got her information from is impossible to say, but what is very clear is that person had been there before the 1750 fire which destroyed the inhabitable part. To judge by the 'angle' of the description they had been high status servants.

"So we set out in a coach, the two ladies being seated in front and myself with the back to the horses; and it was quite dark by the time we arrived at the foot of the castle hill, for it was the dead of winter, and the snow was on the ground; however, there were lamps fixed among the trees all along the private road up to the castle, and there were lights upon the towers, which shone as beacons far and near, for it was a great day at the castle. The horses, though we had four, had hard work to drag us up the snowy path; however, we got up in time, and passing under the gateway, we found ourselves in this court.

But Oh! my children, how different did it then show to what it does now, being littered with splendid equipages, and sounding with the rattling of wheels and the voices of coachmen and grooms calling to each other, and blazing with lights from almost every window. There was such a bustle among the carriages, that we could not drive up to the principal door for some time, and during that delay I had abundance of leisure to look about me.

The keep stood as it does now, a huge and gloomy monument of past days: but all that portion of the castle which extends before you, my dear children, was alive with the bustle and stir of persons bent on pleasure and little thinking of the various changes and chances to which poor human nature is liable, in its passage through this present life; for this my children is not our resting place. How many generations have these old walls beheld, and how many more may it yet be before these rugged towers are entirely mingled with the dust from which they were taken. The oriel windows, the stone frames of which are still so nearly entire, were at that time filled with painted glass, through which the lights which were within emitted rays of various tincture. And the sounds of merry voices and of harps and viols, issued from every doorway.

At length, having drawn up to the steps of the portico, my ladies were handed out by a young gentleman wearing an embroidered waistcoat, with deep pockets and a big whig and sword, and I was driven on to another door, where I was helped out by a footboy, who shewed me the way to the housekeepers room, a square chamber, which, as well as the butler's pantry, and other offices lay in the space under the great hall. Such a figure as was that housekeeper could not be met with in these days, unless it might be on some old tapestried wall: what bustle was she in, with her huge bunch of keys hanging to her girdle by a strong chain of steel.

There were refreshments laid out in every corner of the room, and when I had taken some, I was turned over to a housemaid, who looked as old and antiquated as the housekeeper herself, and by her I was led to the chamber my ladies were to occupy. All vestiges of that chamber and the narrow passage and staircase which led to it, are quite passed away; but I remember the place as well as if I had visited it but yesterday. It was a wide low room, and there was a little closet in it, and it was hung with a tarnished paper, which looked like a cut velvet. And there were huge stout backed chairs, and a large toilet set with Indian dressing boxes.

There was a bright fire in the grate, and whilst the housemaid assisted me to set everything in order for my ladies, she informed me she had lived forty years in the castle, and hoped to finish her days in it. She spoke of her lord and his family, as if there were none in the land that could compare with them. That attachment of the servant to the master is more rare now, than it was in the days that are past; not that human nature is any worse than it was then, but because there has lately arisen in society a spirit of independence, by which all those ancient ties of affection are weakened; and society is hastening to that state of dissolution which, as in the material world, so in the political, must forerun a new order of things ...

Having prepared every thing for my ladies, when they should choose to retire, she asked if I would like to accompany her to see some of the curiosities of the castle, and to look at the company, who had by this time begun to dance. Nothing pleased me more than this proposal; and she, taking a light in her hand, led me all round the chambers, and into the parlours, keeping the great hall, where the company was assembled for the last. Oh! How my were my young eyes dazzled with the splendours which I beheld, for all these things go by comparison; and the eye may be as soon spoilt for admiring fine things, as the taste for enjoying good food. I have seen many noble palaces since that day; but never have I admired any as I did Dudley Castle, when led round it by that faithful and attached housemaid...

I wish, however, that I could bring before you, as it were in pictures, the curious old-fashioned ornaments and pieces of furniture which I saw in the castle. There was not a window which was sashed, but all were casement, in stone frames, many of the panes in coloured glass. And there was scarce one chamber on the same parallel with another, but there was a step to go up or a step to go down to each of these; then the chimney-pieces, being mostly of carved wood or stone, where so high that I could hardly reach to the mantle shelves, when standing on tiptoe; and instead of grates as we have now, there were mostly dogs upon the hearth, such as you, I think, have never seen. Then the chairs were of such a size, that two of the present sort would stand in the room of one, and the doors, though very thick and substantial, were each an inch or two from the floor, so that the wind whistled all along the passages, rattling and shaking the casements, and often making (as my conductor informed me) a mournful melody when not mingled as it was that night, with the sounds of voices, and musical instruments; for as she told me, the castle was even then but seldom visited by the family, and occupied only, excepting on extraordinary occasions, by a few servants. "Nevertheless", said she "it is very pleasant here in the summer season, although there are but three or four of us in this wide mansion. And often times when the country below is hid in smoke, we breath an air as pure as it were so many eagles on the pinnacle of a rock....

I imagine that, even at that time, the lord of the castle had removed the greater part of the most valuable pictures from thence; nevertheless there were many hanging here and there upon the walls, which pleased my young fancy, and one especially in the state bed-room, which was the room above the dining room, having the same oval windows, the stone frames of which you now see. It was a hard rude painting, the colours being much faded, but it represented a lady and a knight with a numerous assemblage of sons and daughters of all ages, from the babe on the mothers lap to the son just setting forth upon the stage of busy life, and assuming the airs of manhood; the towers of Dudley Castle arose in the distance, although their outline could hardly be traced, for the painting was on boards, and empannelled in the wainscot; the lady was seated on a bank of flowers, *and her husband was looking upon her with such an expression of love and confidence, as the tender father and husband often bestows on the mother of his children, and the dutiful honourable wife.*

The dresses seemed as if they had belonged to ages past, perhaps to the time of Elizabeth; but , be that as it may, the picture represented a domestic scene, in which the beautiful and brave, the noble and the delicate, had lived, and moved, and felt, and acted years before even I had entered into existence. And how many bitter and mournful scenes must have taken place before these domestic ties had all been broken, and every individual forming one in that faded group had been committed to the dust... I was, as I said, particularly taken with this family picture, and would willingly have known the names of the persons delineated therein, but the housemaid could not tell me; and because the dancing had commenced in the great hall, and the servants had leave to look on, she was impatient to conduct me thither.

There were three great doors opening from the gallery above into the hall; at one of these, all the servants maids were standing, and I took my place among them. I can hardly tell how to describe this hall to you, unless by saying that the roof was arched and groined not unlike that of some ancient church which you may have seen and it had large and lofty windows pointed and carved in that fashion called Gothic [The windows in the Great Hall were square not pointed. JAH]. *It was illuminated with many candles in sconces of brass hanging from the ceiling, and every corner of it, wide as it was, was as bright as the day. There was a gallery at the further end of it filled with musicians, and foremost was an old harper from Wales, who used in those days to travel the country with his harp on his back, ever presenting himself at the door of that house where feasts and merry makings might be expected. Such as are now seldom to be seen in Wales itself, how much less frequently then in this country. But he led the band, sweeping the strings with high enthusiasm, and keeping up the spirit of those who accompanied him with pipe and tabor and violin, while the hall rocked beneath the quick and measured steps of the gay company who were engaged in the dance; for the assembly was large, and their hearts seemed to be devoted to mirth,,,,*

But I have before me still the figures of that gay and distinguished company, for it consisted of the nobles of the land with their families; the ladies shone with glossy silks and jewels, and the gentlemen with embroidery, and gold and silver lace. The dresses at that time were extremely splendid, and it may be fancy, or it may be not, but I do not think that I ever in those days see faces so fair as some of those which shone that night in that old hall..."

William took his seat in the House of Lords on the 2nd May 1735, but he did not live very long, and died unmarried in 1740 [243].

Figure 47: Drawing of castle from the East, Burgher, 1686. Source: Dudley Art Gallery.

Ferdinando Dudley Lea, 1740-1757: 31st Baron of Dudley

With the death of William Ward the barony was split, and the Dudley part reverted to Frances, the sister of William Ward. Frances married William Lea of Halesowen Grange, and they had an only child, a boy called Ferdinando. Ferdinando was a friend and relation of William Shenstone, the poet and Landscape Gardener who lived across the valley at The Leasowes. In 1739 Ferdinando was in London, as William Shenstone records that he was 'introduced to congenial society' by his lordship. They regularly attended George's Coffee House together [244].

After 1746 Shenstone spent most of his time at home in The Leasowes, and the two friends often met. William described some of Ferdinando's adventures with him in his letters. Ferdinando had an alliance with a Mrs Rock and in the August of 1753 they were staying at the Leasowes. The next morning Mrs Rock tried to encourage Lord Dudley to put some clothes on, which annoyed his lordship, and he swore if the devil came in he would not change. At that instant Lord Temple appeared with a guest and caught Ferdinando in his nightcap and gown [245]. William was amused at some of his friends bedroom antics - a few months later he reported in a letter that Lord Dudley had struck his toe on the bedpost while searching for a chamber pot [246].

It was during this period, on 24th July 1750, that the domestic part of Dudley Castle caught fire. One of the stories of how it happened was that coiners had taken up lodging there, and a timber had caught light. The conflagration ripped through the rest of the buildings. The more observant noticed that the fire started in several different places, and suggested that it was done on purpose by a person or persons who had objections to the baron. Whatever, it burnt for nearly three days according to the Parish Records, and it was so hot that few would risk putting it out. When the fire eventually burnt out all that was left was a ruin.

Figure 48: Reconstruction painting of the burning of Dudley Castle, 1750, by Paul Whitehouse.

Ferdinando died on 21st October 1757, still unmarried, and the lordship after him was divided amongst a few of his kinsmen. After his time the Barony of Dudley, after a period of nearly 700 years, for all intents and purposes fell into abeyance. It was ironic that the swansong of the castle heralded the end of the lordship.

8. Layout of Dudley Castle

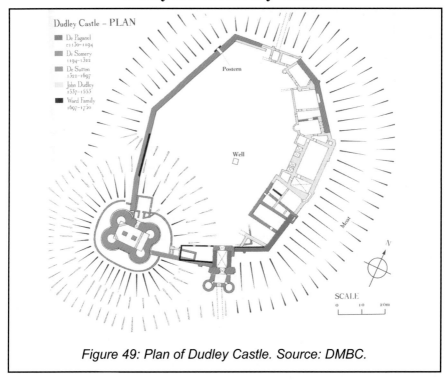

Figure 49: Plan of Dudley Castle. Source: DMBC.

This section will take a walk around the castle in a way that a visitor may go, highlighting the varying structures that they might like to know about.

The Elizabethan Gatehouse

First we start at the Elizabethan Lower Gatehouse at the top of the steep steps that lead up into the Castle itself. The original route that led up to this gatehouse must have been steep enough, why it has been cut away and re-placed with even steeper steps is unknown.

The Lower Gatehouse is the poorest build in the castle, and legend has it that it was built for Queen Elizabeth's visit in 1575. Although there is no evidence to support this, it is possible. The carriageway that ran under the arch had double doors, and to the left of the arch is a spiral staircase that led up to a room on the first floor. This presumably was where the gate keeper lived. It had a brick fireplace in the east wall and a lavatory in the south west corner. Another chamber was situated above this one, and it could have been used as a bedroom. This room gave access to the wall walk and parapet that once surmounted the gatehouse.

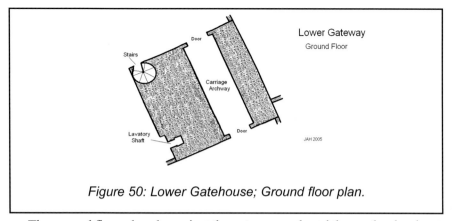

Figure 50: Lower Gatehouse; Ground floor plan.

The ground floor plan shows just the entrance arch and the garderobe shoot.

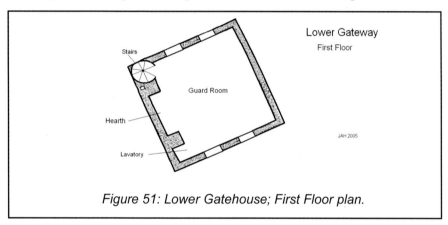

Figure 51: Lower Gatehouse; First Floor plan.

The first floor was where the gatekeeper lived it had a stairway in the north west corner, a fireplace and lavatory.

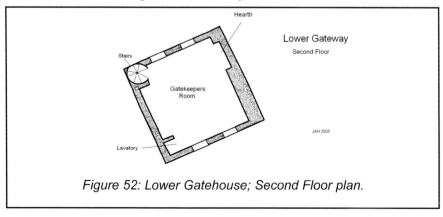

Figure 52: Lower Gatehouse; Second Floor plan.

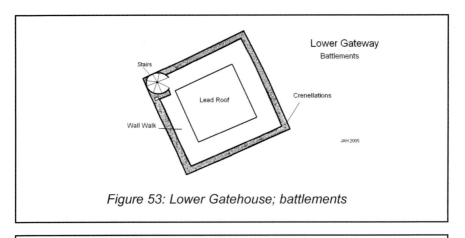

Figure 53: Lower Gatehouse; battlements

Figure 54: Lower Gatehouse.

This photograph of the Lower Gatehouse was taken in 2006.

East Watch Tower

To the east of the gatehouse is another, even less substantial, structure. The tower originally had an outside stairway running down from the ground floor to the basement, and it was called a watch tower in early maps. It also is part of the gatehouse build. It is very debatable that it was built for defensive purposes, but it is definitely an eye-catcher.

Figure 55: Tower. This photograph of the tower was taken in 2005.

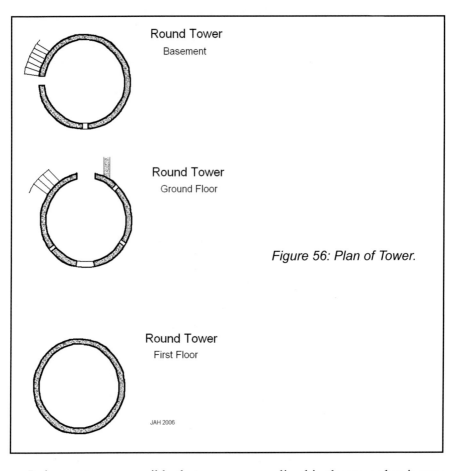

Round Tower
Basement

Round Tower
Ground Floor

Figure 56: Plan of Tower.

Round Tower
First Floor

JAH 2006

It does not seem possible that any one ever lived in the tower but it may have been used for storage.

West Watch Tower

To the west of the gatehouse the defences seem to have all gone. If anything still remains, it must be beneath the nearby cottage. Another structure that replaced the defences was a barn, which lay further west in the 18th century.

Path to Triple Gateway

The path then leads up to the main castle defences; the Norman Motte with 13th century Keep lies on the left. It had at least a 20 foot deep moat around it that has since been backfilled. Although many moats are dry, it is possible that the one at Dudley was originally wet, as a water source is recorded by the Triple Gateway. Presumably this would have once flowed all around the castle.

To the right of the Motte is the curtain wall and to the right of this the Triple Gateway.

Triple Gateway

The Triple Gateway is the most complex of any structures within the castle. It is of at least four different phases. The earliest are the parallel walls within the structure which are 12th century, and had been built by the Paganell's. On the ends of these would have originally been Romanesque doorways that we normally associate with churches. On the west side of the vault is a filled-in window. This must also have been on the former phase. When Roger de Somery made changes to the gateway by building two heavily defended portals on either end of the Paganell work, he also lowered the access route. Consequently some of the Paganell foundations appear within the gateway. The vaulting is Somery, as is the murder hole in the top of the vault.

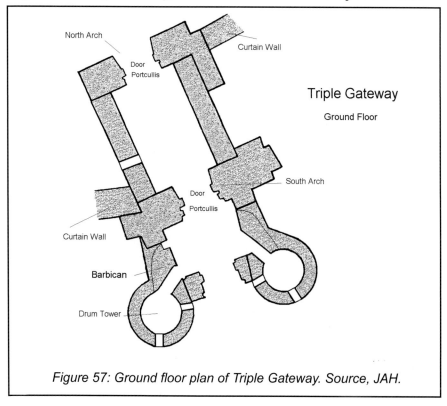

Figure 57: Ground floor plan of Triple Gateway. Source, JAH.

Access to the first floor was through a doorway in the north-east corner, a normal feature of medieval defences. The first floor was where the machinery was kept that raised and lowered the portcullises. Some of the early draw-bridge machinery was also kept in this room, as well as objects to drop on any attacker through the murder hole in the floor.

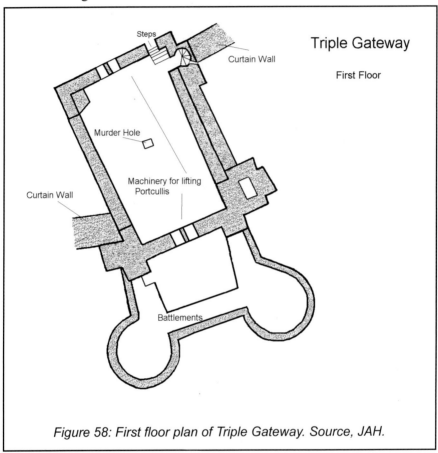

Figure 58: First floor plan of Triple Gateway. Source, JAH.

The second floor was used as the Guard Chamber. Although no trace of a hearth has been found, a lavatory exists on the south east corner.

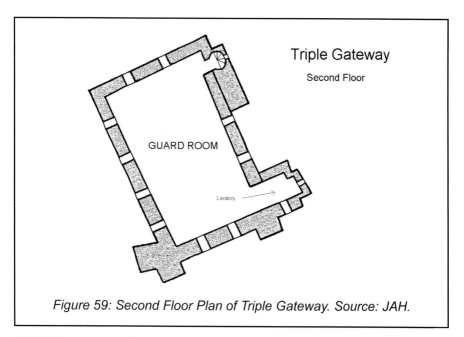

Figure 59: Second Floor Plan of Triple Gateway. Source: JAH.

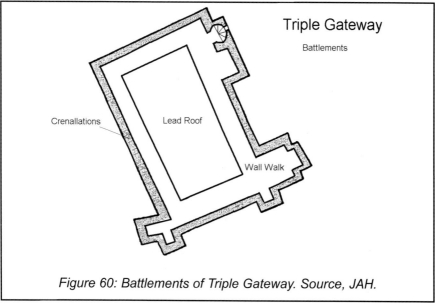

Figure 60: Battlements of Triple Gateway. Source, JAH.

The battlements on the roof of the Triple Gateway gave all around access to the castle defenders. Two corbelled out turrets on the north and south east corners of the structure gave a higher vantage point for any attacks across the moat on the east side [247].

Fig.3 The South View of Dudley Castle (detail) by S & N Buck 1731

During the 15th century John Sutton VI built a barbican, pushing out the front of the main gateway even further southwards. It was built in the moat and there was a tunnel joining up the two drum towers. The moat was extended outwards, and a stone pier was built on to which the drawbridge lay when it was down. This was uncovered in the 1980's during the archaeological excavation of the castle.

John Dudley, in the 16th century, built an arch combining the two towers of the Barbican. This would have led to a modification of the drawbridge. As of yet we do not know what went on. Externally a pier was found in the centre of the moat to support a bridge and a retaining wall on the south side of the moat, though whether this was a permanent bridge or a draw bridge is not known. When the arch was built, he placed three stone coats-of-arms facing the entrance to the gateway. On the left were the Arms of the Sutton family - the Malpas Cross, in the centre were the two lions of the Barony of Dudley - and on the right hand side was the rampant lion of the Talbot Family (kinsman to John Dudley).

Figure 62: The Barbican on the Triple Gateway. Source: D Stevens. Two drum towers at the front guarded a draw bridge which came down on to a pier which stood in the moat.

Once through the Triple Gate, turn to your right. There is a space in front of you and part of the curtain wall. Parts of the 12th century curtain wall were excavated in the 1980's. The mortar of that early period had been reduced to a yellow dust. It is likely that semi-circular stone towers once lined the curtain walls, as the base of one was found by Steve Linnane against the east curtain wall. To the left of this is the chapel and Great Chamber complex [248].

Great Chamber Complex

Initially the great chamber complex was just a rectangular building butting up to the eastern curtain wall. The ground floor was mainly cellarage, or, in the case of the chapel, an undercroft. Interestingly a hearth was later inserted in the under croft, which suggests that it was used as a dwelling place. The greatest change in this block was the insertion of a north-south wall, dividing the Great Chamber section into four rooms, and the chapel, in which the vaulted floor was removed in the 16th century and replaced in brick. The old encaustic tiles on the chapel floor were dumped in the base of the stair well next door, making it un-useable.

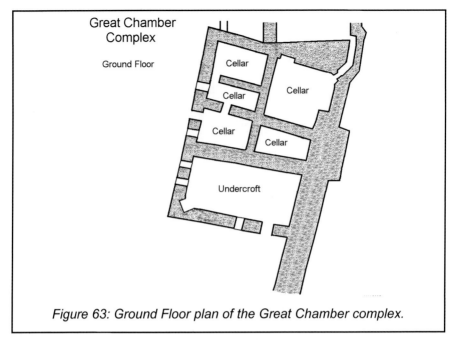

Figure 63: Ground Floor plan of the Great Chamber complex.

The first floor was originally the Great Chamber, with a central hearth in the north wall. John Dudley built a second floor to the building and moved the Great Chamber up a storey. The first floor was divided into two separate chambers and a stair well. The lavatory still remained within the body of the curtain wall.

Figure 64: The Great Chamber

Figure 65: The Castle Chapel

Figure 66: The Great Bedroom

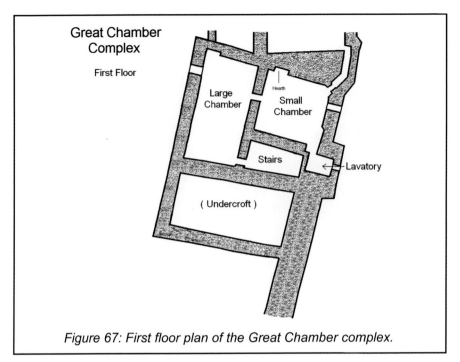

Figure 67: First floor plan of the Great Chamber complex.

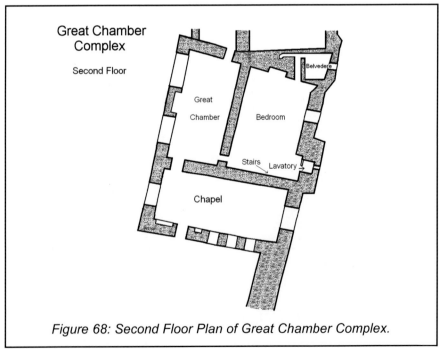

Figure 68: Second Floor Plan of Great Chamber Complex.

John Dudley's second floor comprised a great chamber in the east with access to the castle chapel. The stair well and the lavatory existed on the south east side and a bedroom to the north east, with access through to a belvedere, or look out tower to the north east of this room. The chapel had a blind arcade on the south side with two alcoves, one to the east and another to the west; they would have served as a piscina, where the vessels were cleaned after Mass, and a stoup used by the congregation to soak their fingers on entering the chapel.

To the north of the Great Chamber complex is the Renaissance Range. This was composed of the service area to the north and the public part of the castle to the south.

Renaissance Range

The Renaissance Range was built by Sir William Sharrington in the 1540's for John Dudley, and most of the pre-existing architecture was destroyed. Colin Johnson created a reconstruction of the layout of the castle (through a computerised walk) for Queen Elizabeth II's visit in 1994. The still images on the following pages were taken from this display.

Figure 69. Renaissance Range.Sir William Sharrington demolished many of the older buildings at Dudley Castle and constructed this 'new' style of building - probably the first Italianate structure in the West Midlands.

134

Opposite page
Figure 70: The kitchen had two huge hearths and would have served both the needs for the family and residents as well as banquets. Computer image by Colin Johnson, Image Interactive.

Figure 71: The Servery. Servants would fetch food from the service hatch on the left and deliver it to the Private Dining Room or Great Hall by the steps in front. Computer image by Colin Johnson, Image Interactive.

Next page
Figure 72: The Great Hall looking south. The musicians were said to play in a gallery above the dais at the end of the room, not shown in this image. Computer image by Colin Johnson, Image Interactive.

Figure 73: The Great Hall looking north. The main entrance to the hall was from the north with a 'spyhole' at an upper level. Computer image by Colin Johnson, Image Interactive.

Figure 74: The Chapel looking east which in this period had a very plain appearance. Computer image by Colin Johnson, Image Interactive.

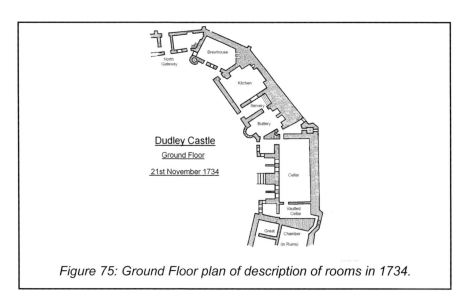

Figure 75: Ground Floor plan of description of rooms in 1734.

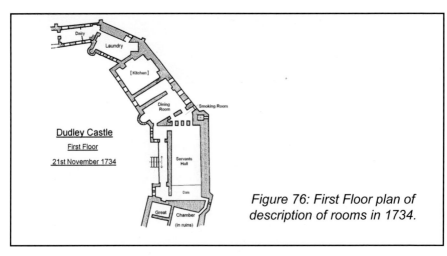

Figure 76: First Floor plan of description of rooms in 1734.

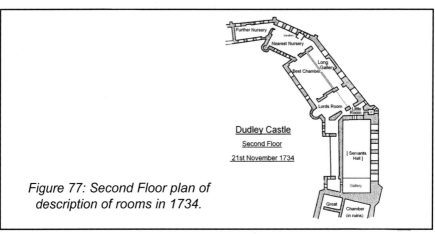

Figure 77: Second Floor plan of description of rooms in 1734.

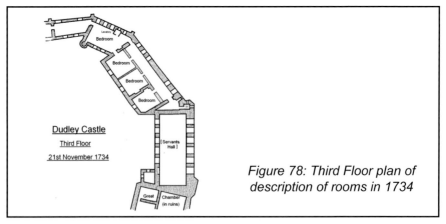

Figure 78: Third Floor plan of description of rooms in 1734

To go with this is an 'Account of Goods in the Castle taken on 21st November 1734' which has recently been found. This account lists articles in various rooms of the castle. Why this was made is not clear, but the important point about it is that most inventories were made the same way, that is, by listing the articles as one moved from room to room.

1) The first room is the kitchen, with appropriate fireplace utensils, boilers and cisterns.

2) The second room is called the Buttery. This is what Mrs Sherwood later called the Housekeepers Chamber, situated on the ground floor, with the bay window. A coffer and table were recorded in this room.

3) The third room leads from the Buttery, and was called the Servants Hall. This was most certainly the Great Hall, with its Long Table, benches, suits of armour, bills and hatchments (Coats-of-Arms).

4) From the hall one climbed the stairs in the north-west corner to the first floor, and entered the Smoking Room. This had four easy chairs in it.

5) This then led in turn into the Dining Room. No table was recorded in this room, which suggests that the habit of eating here had ceased. This is one of the factors which suggest that the use of the castle was growing less.

6) Stairs led to the second floor. This was the best chamber or master bedroom. A bed was obviously situated here.

7) This led to the Long Gallery, with its fire grate and chairs.

8) The little room at the end of the gallery seems likely to have been the upper gallery, with the spy hole into the Great Hall.

9) The Lords Room was used as a Drawing Room.

The next two items appear to be in reverse order, probably by entering the next section from the Long Gallery.

10) The Further Nursery is next, with five beds. This must have been the room in the north gate.

11) The Nearest Nursery, with tables, chairs and drawers, would have been next to the Long Gallery. From here the surveyor went down the Octagon Tower to the first floor.

12) The room beneath on the first floor was called the dairy. It only had a cheese press in it in 1734.

13) The next room was the Laundry Room. It included: a grate, an iron furnace, a pastry plate, a coffer, bench and dresser and lay next to the North gateway.

14) The next room was on the ground floor and was the Brew House, with its copper furnace that was situated close to the entrance way to the kitchen where we began. [249]

Buttery

This is the most important room architecturally, as Sir William Shenstone left a 12th century wall in place. In the north wall you will notice a huge doorway and a blocked up window. This relates to the Paganell phase. It is very large, and gives us some idea of how well the Paganell castle was constructed. It probably related to a kitchen block, as Norman living quarters were normally at first floor level.

Figure 79: Blocked doorway in Butler's Pantry. This feature relates to the 12th century and the time of the Paganell's. As the living quarters of the inhabitants was on the second storey it was possibly this was the entrance way to an ancillary building: Kitchens, Stables etc.

Bailey

From the Renaissance Range, walk along the western edge of the curtain wall, past the demolished building next to the north gate, until you come to a doorway in the wall. This is the place where a postern gate once stood, where the Royalists charged down to attack the Parliamentarians defending the Priory during the Civil War. Walking on you will notice features within the wall - these probably belonged to Sir William Sharrington's rebuild in the 16th century.

Most of the bailey area has yet to be archaeologically excavated, but occasionally in hot summers the grass dies in areas where there are walls beneath it.

Figure 80: Crop marks in Bailey. Source: DMBC.

Hidden features still appear as scorch marks in the Bailey. These represent the walls of buried features not yet excavated. The feature in the photograph has an apsidal end. It may represent a chapel built earlier than the chapel in the Great Chamber.

Walk up the path to the Keep, and go through the entrance way.

Keep

What kind of stone structure was built at Dudley Castle in the early phase we are not sure about. The mid 12th century castles show great square keeps or circular shell keeps on top of or in place of the mottes. It is unlikely that Dudley had one of these. The motte top, although it had been reduced, was not reduced enough to fit one of these on the top. Perhaps a stone tower once stood there. That there was something on the motte can be proven by the 12th century bridge abutment excavated below the motte and up against the west curtain wall.

The present Keep was constructed in the 1260's. It is an immense feature that was very different in style to the rest of the keep's constructed in the 13th century. The entrance way was protected by a portcullis and a huge oak door. On the south side of the ground floor was a hearth, which suggests that this floor was used as a kitchen prior to the building of the kitchen outside. A garderobe or lavatory is in the north west drum tower, and a stairway (for the servants) in the north east drum tower. Two huge pillars supported the first floor. These appear to have been replaced by two thin walls in John Dudley's changes to the complex in the mid 16th century. The main access to the first floor was on the left side of the entrance way. The Keep was probably the home of the Constable of the castle.

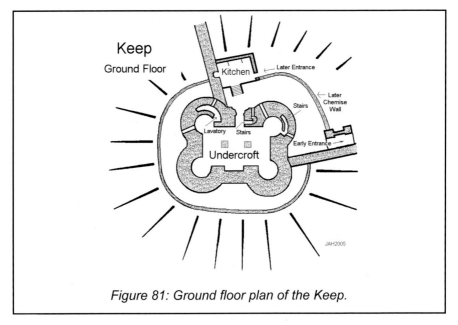

Figure 81: Ground floor plan of the Keep.

The first floor of the Keep was a hall, with the west end containing private chambers. A large fireplace and a lavatory were within the hall.

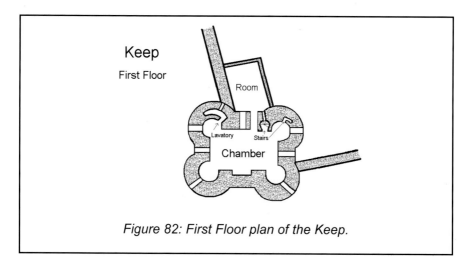

Figure 82: First Floor plan of the Keep.

The second floor of the Keep were the battlements, rising to a fighting platform on a third floor on the drum towers.

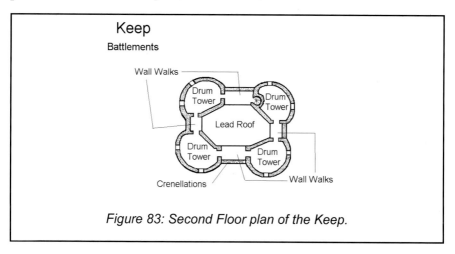

Figure 83: Second Floor plan of the Keep.

The original Keep Gatehouse lay on the east of the motte. It originally had a stairway up to the motte within it, but at a later date the stairway was withdrawn to the east, so that a plank floor over a large open space could be lifted in times of attack within the structure, making it inaccessible [250].

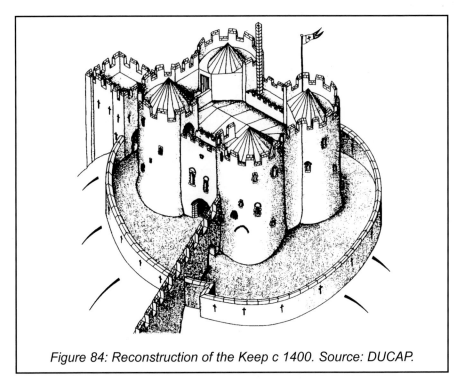

Figure 84: Reconstruction of the Keep c 1400. Source: DUCAP.

On the Bailey side of the keep is a square foundation - this is the Kitchen Annex.

Kitchen Annex

John Sutton VI also had a single storey kitchen built up against the keep on the motte top. This was a square structure with a central fireplace. A new access up to the keep was added to by entering a door in the kitchen's south east corner. The old access, along the south curtain wall, was presumably still available for the gentry to use. The hearth appeared to have had constant use, proven by the wear and tear that had occurred to it, and the massive amount of animal bones that had been tipped down the motte side below the structure.

When John Dudley began a refurbishment in the middle of the 16th century, he placed the hearth on the north wall and created a second floor, possibly with access into the keep. The wall bread oven was closed and the east door was blocked. He also completed the back filling of the original internal moat around the motte.

During the Civil War the annex was used as a smithy to repair and make weapons of war. The evidence of hammer scale and holes to hold machinery was found in the kitchen floor during excavation. The Keep was also used in this way during the war, as lead was found embedded in a hole dug in the ground floor Keep hearth; it got there presumably during the process of making shot [251].

17th Century Civil War Sleighting

Although Sir William Brereton argued that the castle could be held by a Parliamentary garrison in 1646, the order was given to destroy the fortifications, and this work started in 1647. The chief structures they pinpointed for demolition were the gatehouse and the keep, but other areas were also pulled down, though what the reason was for these is not quite clear. According to a drawing by Burgher in 1686, forty years later, they pulled down the whole of the Great Chamber complex and Chapel, but left the curtain wall, dilapidated - but still up! The building between the chapel and the Triple Gateway was completely gone, even to the extent of having the foundations robbed out of the trenches. Most of the Barbican on the Triple Gateway was demolished, and the south facing wall on the first and second floors of the main block itself were pulled out leaving just a shell left.

The curtain wall between the Triple Gateway and the keep was reduced to ground level. The south, east and west walls of the Keep were pulled down. As the kitchen annex had been used as an armoury during the Royalist campaign, this was also demolished - in fact so well that no one had any idea it was there until the archaeological excavation revealed it in 1985. The west curtain wall with its wall walk was also pulled down. As Sharrington had built a range of buildings up against this, they were somewhat unstable having the whole of their west walls demolished, so they also came down. Surprisingly, they left the north gate. Why they pulled the stair tower to the north east of the Great Hall down is unclear, unless of course it had been used as an observation post during the sieges.

The only buildings they left were those dwellings that we call the Sharrington Range. It is difficult to say who did the slighting, but it may have been the military, given in the main that the defendable parts of the castle were made defunct. They had no intentions of clearing the whole of the site, which probably suggest that they had a time-limit on the destruction and it seems likely that they were pulled off the job before they had finished.

Now walk back down the path to the stable block, now "The Grey Lady", a licensed premises.

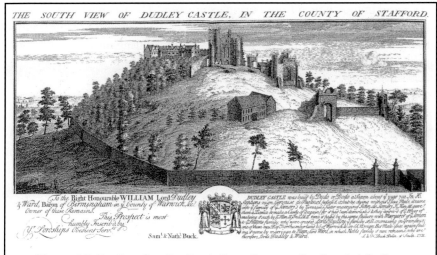

THE SOUTH VIEW OF DUDLEY CASTLE, IN THE COUNTY OF STAFFORD.

Figure 85: Dudley Castle, Buck Bros Source: Dudley Art Gallery.

Post Civil War Re-build: Stable Block

There must have been some tidy-up of the site after the demolition of the castle defences, but what this was is not clear. By the 18th century the castle was in some use again. The eastern foundations of the west wall buildings were cleared out, and a sunken walk was constructed along them. This appears to have been a garden feature placed here before the curtain wall was rebuilt. In the Buck brother's drawing of the castle in 1731, a stable block appears to have been built between the Triple Gateway and the old Gatehouse to the Keep [252].

The Stable Block is an irregular rectangle, with fine detailing on the north wall facing into the bailey. This building was constructed with care, and seems to imply a desire to bring back the days before the Civil War destruction. It is possible that if time and money had been forthcoming a re-building scheme would have ended up replacing all the structures in the western bailey wall. The fact that it was used as a stable and not a dwelling was revealed in the archaeological evidence on the floor, being a brick surface on the southern side and a stepped paved floor on the north side. This is a normal floor plan for a stable. The first floor may have been used as a hay loft, but a dwelling for a castle operative like an ostler is not out of order, with access from the outside in the west wall, though there does not appear to be a fireplace to support this! [253].

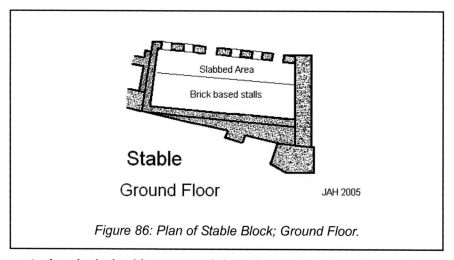

Figure 86: Plan of Stable Block; Ground Floor.

Archaeological evidence proved that this was indeed an eighteenth century stable.

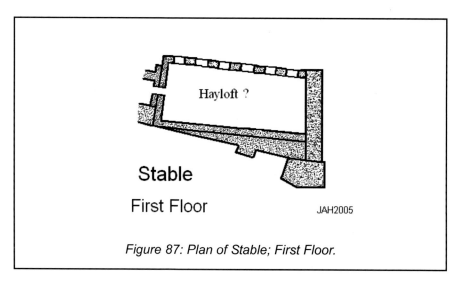

Figure 87: Plan of Stable; First Floor.

Figure 88: Photograph of Stable Block.

Conclusion

After the 1750's fire some of the unstable walls were pulled down, and the castle became abandoned. Early drawings show animals grazing amongst the piles of stone, which suggest it was let out for pasture. These also showed a closed gate below Castle Hill, so it remained a private estate. As time went by, however, interest began to grow in such places, and travellers and townspeople began to gain access to visit it. It was probably because of this use that in 1810 the Earl of Dudley started to clear up the site; part of this work was the rebuilding of part of the north eastern drum tower in the keep. Another area he seems to have worked on was the chapel undercroft, which is shown in ruins in early sketches. A lot of the stone work was cleared away, and it seems that he began to plant ivy around the walls to make it look like a romantic ruin.

The castle became a focal point during the 19th century, and the Castle Fetes drew crowds into the Bailey. In 1936 the Earl of Dudley in conjunction with Bristol Zoo opened Dudley Zoo, and placed the animals in purpose-built constructions designed by the well known architect Bertold Lubetkin around the castle. Many people visited the Zoo in the 20th century and wandered into the castle ruins, but it was not until the 1980's that the castle underwent a restoration and archaeological excavation. By the end of the century it became a feature in its own right, even having her Majesty Queen Elizabeth open up the Interpretation Centre under the Great Hall and Great Chamber blocks in 1994.

What will happen to the castle in the future no one knows, but for now it can sleep peacefully with the understanding that a number of people care for it.

Acknowledgements

I am indebted to a number of people and organisations for their help and advice - those historians who added so much knowledge of the subject, especially Henry Grazebrook, whose "The Barony of Dudley" opened the door to further study, and W F Carter, who continued the hunt in the 1940's. But it is my living colleagues who deserve most of my thanks: Steve Linnane, Stephanie Ratkai, Colin Johnson, Joan Tyson, Adrian Durkin and Graham Worton; Kevin Bridgewater supplied me with some of the original documentation, and Margery Dudley Wright, supplied me with information about Picquigny; Peter Suddock from Dudley Zoo, provided help in getting photographs of the site, and Neil Ludlow and Peter Boland did the reconstruction drawings, which are copyright to Dudley Metropolitan Borough Council. Neil Lang took the cover photograph, and Roger Dodsworth gave me permission to use the paintings and drawings from Dudley Art Gallery; Birmingham Reference Library for two images of the castle; the National Portrait Gallery for the pictures of John Dudley and Queen Elizabeth, Bibliotheque nationale de France for the illustration of the Battle of Crecy, British Library for the Execution of Hugh Despencer, Burrell Collection of Glasgow for the Coat-of-Arms of the Barony of Dudley and the Mary Rose Trust for Cowdray's painting of the Battle of the Solent and John Dudley's Pewter Plate. I also need to thank Mike Hessey who turned my ideas into publishable material. Finally, the now defunct Dudley Castle Archaeological Project (DUCAP), without whom I would ever have been given the opportunity to work on the castle, and Dudley Metropolitan Borough Council my employers.

No doubt there are many others that I need to thank whose names are now lost in time. Any mistakes in this work are my own, and therefore do not blame my friends and colleagues.

Bibliography

Barrow, G W S (1956), Feudal Britain, Arnold. London.

Beer, Barrett L (1973), Northumberland; The Political Career of John Dudley, Earl of Warwick and Duke of Northumberland, Kent State Univ. Ohio.

Beresford, W (c 1878), Diocesan Histories: Lichfield, SPCK, London.

Blanom, William Henry, The Barons War.

Blocksidge, E (1885), Guide to Dudley Castle and Priory, Dudley.

Bingham, Charlotte (1973), The Life and Times Of Edward 1st, London.

Bryant, A (1963), The Storey of England, Vol.2. The Age of Chivalry, London.

Chandler & Hannah (1949), Dudley as it was and is today, Dudley.

Carter, W F (1962), Additions to Grazebrook's The Barons of Dudley

Chancellor, John (1979), Strongholds of the Realm.

Collections for a History of Staffordshire, The Staffordshire Record Society, William Salt Library:; including:- Close Rolls, Mag Reg, Licences & Mem Rolls.

Colvin (1951), The White Canons of England, Oxford.

Coley, Ellis & Bandinel (1885) Monisticum V.

Dicto, Radulf de, Opera Historica, Vol II.

Domesday Book: Worcestershire, Warwickshire, Staffordshire, Shropshire, Northamptonshire, Rutland, Buckinghamshire, Oxfordshire, Surrey. Phillimore, Chichester.

Duckett, G W (1888), Charters and Records of the Abbey of Cluni, Vols I & II, Lewes.

Dudley, C D M (1971), The Dudley Family.

Dudley Estate Papers:- Dudley Archive.

Dugdale, Sir William (1637), Monasticon Anglicanum, William Salt Collection.

Dugdale, Sir William (1675), The Baronage of England.

Falkus, Gilla (1981), The Life and Times of Edward IV, Weidenfield & Nicolson.

Fraser, Antonia (1969), Mary, Queen of Scots, London.

Forester, Thomas (trans 1854), The Chronicle of Florence of Worcester, London.

Grazebrook, H S (1888), The Barons of Dudley, Vol IX, Stafford.

Green, J (1976), A Short History of the English People, London

Gross, A J (1991), King's Lordship in the County of Stafford 1312-1322, Midland History,Vol.XVI.

Grose, Francis (1776), Antiquities of England and Wales, Vol. 6.

Guttery, D R (1950), The Two John's: Patron and Parson, Brierley Hill.

Harwood, Thomas (1820), Erdeswick's A History of Staffordshire.

Hemingway, John (trans), The Letterbook of Sir William Brereton referring to the Time of the Leaguers at Dudley and Tutbury Castles and Lichfield Close; 4th April to 19th May 1645, unpublished.

Hemingway, John, (2005) An Illustrated Chronicle of the Cluniac Priory of Saint James, Dudley, Friends of Priory Park.

Holinshead, Chronicles, Vol. III.

Hunt, John Robert (1994), Lordship and the Landscape; A Documentary and Archaeological study of the Honor of Dudley, c 1066-1322, Ph D Thesis, University of Birmingham.

Hutton, W H (1901) [Ed], Simon de Montfort and his cause; 1251-1266, London.

Kendall, P M (1973), Warwick the Kingmaker and the Wars of the Roses.

King, Peter (2002), Dud Dudley, Historical Metallurgy.

Knightly, Charles, The Story of England.

Linnane, Steve (1993), Dudley Castle Dissected. The Stables, in Ramparts Vol. 4, 1st Edition, Dudley.

Linnane, Steve (1998), The Kitchen Annex in Ramparts, Vol. 9,1st Edition, Dudley.

Linnane, Steve (1993), Dudley Castle Dissected; The Keep in Ramparts Vol. 4, 2nd Edition, Dudley.

Linnane, Steve (1997), Dudley Castle Dissected; Triple Gate in Ramparts, Vol. 8, 2nd Edition, Dudley.

Linnane, Steve (2004), The Chapel and Great Chamber in Ramparts, Vol.15, No.2, Dudley.

Lisle, Leopold de, Companions of the Conqueror.

Locock, Martin, Medieval Floor Tiles from St. James's Priory, Dudley, unpublished.

Macdonald, Alec (1943), Worcester in English History, London.

Mander, Gerald P (1962), Appendix to Carter's Additions to Grazebrook's The Barons of Dudley

Myers, A R, The Household of Queen Margaret of Anjou, 1452-3.

E Monro Purkis, William Shenstone, Poet and Landscape Gardener.

Nash, T (1782), Collections for a History of Worcestershire, London.

Nichols, John (1823), Progresses of Queen Elizabeth, Society of Antiquiries, London.

Nicholson, R (1974), Scotland in the Middle Ages, Edinburgh.

Pagett, T & Barker, P (1988), Romanesque Carvings from St John the Baptist Church, Hagley and Dudley Priory, in Trans. Worc. Arch. Soc., Third Ser. Vol II.

Payton, J (1794), An Authentic History and Description of the Castle & Priory of Dudley chiefly compiled from the works of Leland, Erdeswick, Plott, Gross etc, Dudley.

Radford, C A R (1940), Dudley Priory in Antiquaries Journal ,XX.

Ratcliff, O (1900), The History and Antiquities of Newport Pagnell Hundred, Olney.

Razi, Z (1980), Life and Death in a Medieval Parish, Cambridge.

Records of Dudley in the Public Record Office, Vol I, II, III, Stafford.

Red Book of the Exchequer, Vol I, II, III, London.

Rollason, A A (1930), Chronological Events in the History of Dudley, 700~1500, Dudley.

Roper, J (1980), Four Early Vicars of Dudley, Dudley.

Savage, A (1982), Anglo-Saxon Chronicles, London.

Sergeant, H (1952-1957) Worcestershire Historical Society.

Sherwood, Mrs (1832), Dudley Castle.

State Papers: Domestic.

Stenton, F (1971), Anglo-Saxon England, Oxford.

Storey, R L (1986), The End of the House of Lancaster, 2nd Edition.

Tilley, R (1983), A History of St Edmunds Church, Dudley.

Twamley, O (1867), History of Dudley Castle and Priory, London.

Tyson, Joan. (1999) After the Civil War in Ramparts, Vol. 10, First Edition, Dudley.

Underhill, E A (1942), The Story of the Ancient Manor of Sedgley, Sedgley.

Victoria County History: Staffordshire, Warwickshire, Worcestershire, North-amptonshire.

Warringer, John (1975), The Paston Letters, London.

Weaver, J R H (1908), The Chronicles of John of Worcester, 1118-1140, Oxford.

Williams, Marjorie (1939), Letters of William Shenstone, Oxford.

Willis~Bund, J W (1894), Inquisitions Post Mortem, Worcester.

Wrottesley, (1887), Military Service as Performed by Staffordshire Tenants, Stafford.

Wrottesley, Crecy to Calais Vol. XVIII, Salt.

Wrottesley, De Banco Rolls, Salt.

Glossary

Abutment: Part of a wall which takes the thrust of an arch.

Advowson: The right of a person or institution to choose the parish priest. The early churches were built and funded by private individuals who had the right to say who should take services there.

Adventurer: A soldier-of-fortune who fights for profit.

Affinity: The relationship between a great lord and a lesser lord.

Aid: A gift from a free tenant to his king. The king could demand an aid: 1. for a ransom, 2. when his eldest son was knighted, or 3. when his daughter was married.

Armada: A great fleet of ships.

Attorney-General: Chief legal officer of the king.

Apse: A semi-circular area at the eastern end of the church.

Assart: An enclosure of woodland and waste for agricultural purposes.

Barons: The fifth rank of peerage, also termed Lord.

Booty: Property acquired by taking it off its owner.

Borders: A cottager who was called to perform agricultural or manual services.

Burgess: A person who lives in a borough. He normal has the right to buy and sell things. Trading outside a borough was technically illegal. His house and garden was known as a burgess plot.

Calendar: The medieval year ran from Old New Years Day, March 25th (also called Lady Day) to March 24th. So for instance their January 1346 would be our January 1347. Something of this system survives in the financial year.

Canonised: The making of a holy man into a saint, only a Pope could do this, although there are unofficial 'saints'.

Carucate: From carra - a plough. Although not a standard measurement it approximated to 120 acres. A carucate was divided into 4 virgates (30 acres), which was the normal land holding in the Middle Ages.

Cavalry: A mounted warrior.

Caput: Head of the barony from old French 'cap' for head.

Cell: A subdivision of a whole, the Priory of St James of Dudley was part of the Priory of St Milburga, Much Wenlock.

Chancery: The Court of the Chancellor. It dealt with royal grants and privileges.

Chaplain: A priest in charge of a chapel.

Church: The normal definition of a church is the senior ecclesiastical establishment in a parish.

Chapel: A chapel is inferior to a church and did not have a parish of its own.

Chemise wall: A wall that skirts around the base of another wall.

Clerks: A man who had taken holy orders - a cleric. As these were the only people who could read and write it came to be used for any one with this talent.

Coat-of-Arms: Originally they were symbols pertaining to a family worn on a surcoat over armour.

Coneygre: Coney - rabbit, gre - green. Rabbits were introduced into England in the 12th century but they were called coneys; as they still are in the furrier trade. It was the babies or kittens that were called rabbits! Warrens were in fact any place where small hunted animals were kept.

Court Baron: A manorial Court which enforced the customs of the manor and held every three weeks

Court Leet: A Manorial Court that dealt with minor offences and held twice a year.

Croft: Part of the land attached to a house or tenement.

Currency: The basic currency was the pre-1974 monetary system of pounds (£), shillings(s) and pence (d). Twelve pence was equal to a shilling and twenty shillings equal to a pound.

Curtain Wall: A wall that surrounded the keep and bailey.

Customs of the Manor: Rules that governed the traditions of manors.

Deed: A legal document describing the transference of rights or property from one person or organisation to another.

Demesne: From the French, 'possessing as ones own'. The demesne was the lord's personal holding in contrast to the lands he leased out to his knights.

Deputy Lieutenant: The king's representative in a shire.

Deforcient: A person who keeps out of possession the rightful owner of an estate.

Dower lands: Originally lands a husband gave to his wife on their wedding day, but it came to mean her part of his estate she retained on his death.

Earl: An Anglo-Saxon Aristocrat.

Encaustic Tiles: A fired clay block. The pattern on the surface was made by inserting paler clay into grooves and then covering it with powdered lead. When fired the lead would form a hard transparent coat.

Enfeoffed: To put a tenant in legal possession of a property.

Escheator: A man who collected the revenues when an estate escheated (reverted) to the crown.

Exchequer: The financial section of the royal courts.

Furlong: Originally the amount of land oxen would plough before needing to stop for breath became the lineal measurement of 220 yards.

Fee Tail: Land or an estate that can be inherited.

Feudal: Tenure of land subject to military service.

Heriot: Obligation of a tenant to give as a gift the best animal he has to the lord on his taking up a tenancy.

Herald: The king's heralds kept a list of all coats-of-arms and who had the right to wear them. They still do!

Homage and Fealty: A ceremonial pledge of loyalty and obligation made to a king.

Honour: The rights and responsibilities of a baron as regards his estates and men who serve him.

Infantry: Foot soldiers.

Inquisition Post Mortem: An Inquisition was a court. Post mortem is Latin for after death. The IPM was a sort of inquiry for death duties.

Justiciars: Chief political and judicial officer of the king.

Justice of the Peace: Magistrate within the shires, to make judgements on local offences at the Quarter Session Courts.

Keep: A defended tower within a castle.

Knights: Mounted warriors who had been given land for their service.

Knight's Fees: A feudal tenure which obliged the holder to provide military assistance to his lord.

Latin: The language of the Roman Empire. Adopted by Christians and used all over Europe. Still used in science, law and medicine.

Lay Subsidy: A royal income tax in which church men were exempt.

Lord Lieutenant: The king's representative in the shire and keeper of the shire records.

Litigation: Be a party to a law suite.

Lord Protector: Serves as senior officer of the country in lieu of the king.

Mark: A mark was valued at 13 shillings and 4 pence, 2/3rds of a pound. It was never an actual coin but was widely used as a way of calculating values. A mark constituted about 9 months normal salary in the 13th century.

Manor: An estate held of a baron, who was himself a tenant of the king.

Marshalsea: A royal prison, named after Marshalsea near London.

Marches: The border lands to England of Scotland and Wales.

Men-at-Arms: Infantry warriors who were given land for military service.

Minority: While a person was still underage. They normally came of age when they were twenty one.

Oyer and Terminer: A commission to 'hear and determine' into serious offences.

Palatinate: An area governed by an earl that had a great deal of self rule.

Palisade: A timber fence that encircled a castle.

Pale: The pale was a fence, which in the case of Ireland surrounded Dublin when it was occupied by the English. Any one outside of this area was 'beyond the pale'.

Parish: Originally an estate possessing its own church, later the area that a church was responsible for.

Patronage: The right of a lord to give anyone moral or financial support.

Plaintiff: A person who brings a suit into a court of law.

Plough lands: The cultivated arable strips in the medieval open field system.

Privy Council: The personal council of a king.

Protection: Letters were sent to the kings fighting men saying their property for the duration will be under royal protection,

Rent of Assize: A fixed rent. In an inflationary world like the Middle Ages fixed rents were hated by the landowners and loved by the tenants.

Rolls; Close - Patent - Fine -: Official documents, consisting of a number of separate pieces of parchment stitched together to form a roll.

Royal Edict: A ruling declared by the king.

Scutage: 'Shield Tax'. Fighting duty was gradually commuted to a monetary fine as most kings preferred to employ professional warriors.

Seneschal: A steward.

Sequestration: Confiscation of a person's property.

Sheriff: The king's representative in the shire responsible for law and order.

Sleighted: The castles walls were demolished to make it undefendable.

Steward: Originally a person who personally served the lord but later his chief agent.

Tenement: A house and the farm land that was attached to it.

Vill: A village, but in the Middle Ages, this included all the fields around it that the villagers worked in.

Virgate: A measurement of land, normally 30 acres.

Villein: An independent yeoman farmer.

Wardship: The habit of the king giving the responsibility to another lord of bringing up an underage boy when his father died.

Notes

1. Their actual relationship is unknown, but they could have been younger sons of the Videme or the sons of his brother Jean Hubert. M. Leopolde de Lisle, Companions of the Conqueror/Grazebrook, p 7. /Picquigny and its Castles.
2. Carter, p 23.
3. King Edward had died in the December of 1065 and it appears King Harold had not had time to dispose of them. We know little about Ulf except for the fact that he had a sizeable estate. DB, Bucks.
4. Giles, Ansculf's brother, was also given estates in Buckingham, Berkshire, Oxford and Northampton, but only a fraction of the value of Ansculf's. Victoria County History of Northampton, 1902, p 291-2.
5. Domesday Book; Bucks, Berks, Surrey, Middlesex, Rutland, Oxford, Northampton, Huntingdon. Ansculf was not exactly famous for his generosity. An Englishman called Alaric held Marsh Gibbon both "harshly and wretchedly", according to Domesday. Bradwell had also been dispossessed by the sheriff.
6. Stenton, p 601.
7. Edric escaped to Scotland but in the June of 1070 he made his peace with King William. He was too capable a warrior for the king not to use his skills - he is last heard of fighting for the king in France! Stephenson p 139. Stenton p 603-605 gives a brief description of Edric's campaigns.
8. The modern name, Wrens Nest, for one of these outcrops is a corruption of the Anglo-Saxon - W*rosne*, which means 'the link'. Both Castle Hill and Wrens Nest are links in the Ridgeway, so it was probably the original name for the area.
9. The castle has been considered to be within the manor/estate/parish of Dudley, Worcestershire since 1086 where it is stated as such, DB; Worcestershire. But in reality it was part of Sedgley and in Staffordshire. Why this is so is not altogether clear, but it may have something to do with ownership. Sedgley was a royal estate held by Ansculf; Dudley actually belonged to him. As the king considered the castle to be his property, he probably 'attached' the castle to his estate of Sedgley. There is a narrow strip of land on the west side of the hill, the site of a mill, that has never been part of Sedgley and this makes one think that the hill was traditionally part of Dudley. Also DB Warwick, DB Staffs.
10. Grazebrook, p 7.
11. Savage, p 213. See also Yorkshire families, Yorkshire Archaeological Society, 1973.

12. This may explain why the later Red Book of the Exchequer suggested the Paganell-Somery Honour was acquired through the crown, rather than being hereditary, something one would have expected if the Paganell's had acquired it by marriage. R.B.E. p 269-270.

13. Grazebrook, P.27. Caley, Ellis & Bandinel, p 205.

14. Paganell versus Parles, Staffordshire Pipe Roll of Henry 1.32. (1129-30)/ Paganell re. Wolverhampton- According to Miscellaneous Inquisitions in the Public Record Office Fulke is recorded as holding 30½ acres freehold in Wolverhampton, but that is all. R.of.D. Vol. 3, p 67. It is possible that this was Kings Manor, as King John later took it off Ralph de Somery? The Canons of Wolverhampton had a difficult time during The Anarchy and perhaps more property came to the barony!

15. Ralph had a younger brother called William who married Juliana de Bampton. Their sons Fulke and William were the ancestors of the Paganell's of Bampton and Bridgewater. Grazebrook, p 8.

16. Grazebrook, p 8.

17. Barrow, p 114.

18. Weaver, p 50.

19. Forester, p 50, Grazebrook (Dugdale) p 8.

20. Grazebrook, p 7-8.

21. Manders, p 58.

22. Grazebrook, p 9. As the Paganell's were traditional supporters of Matilda, it may have been in the Beaumont's interest to get the kudos of being related to the "in" people. For general account see Barrow, Feudal Britain, p 114-122.

23. Worcester.

24. Walter's motte and bailey has recently been excavated.

25. It was always safer for a lesser lord to be in a greater lords company. This worked for both of them the lesser lord having the protection and the greater lord having fighting men in his retinue. This is the meaning of the word affinity!

26. Grazebrook, p 9.

27. Dugdale, p 766-8, Manders, p 71.

28. Carter, p 24.

29. Hooper, Nicholas & Bennett Mathew

30. Radulf de Diceto, p 404.

31. Grazebrook, p 8/Pipe Rolls, Roof D, p 69.

32. The atral curves, or the reversed 'S' pattern, of the plough lands can still be made out in some of the property boundaries in Dudley, as can furlong patterns.

33. St Edmund, king and martyr, was an 11th century king of East Anglia killed by the Danes. Church's tended to be dedicated to him up to the Norman Conquest but not after. Even so it is a rare dedication in the west midlands and might have been chosen by an Anglo-Saxon thegn of Dudley, with East Anglian antecedents. It is likely that the town of Dudley was originally called Upton or Overton, which was the opposite of the place-name Netherton.

34. The dedication is later than 1173 - the year Thomas was canonised by the Pope, but earlier than 1180, when first mentioned in a charter.

35. Roper, p i (1980).

36. Dugdale, Vol. lid, p 907 / Beresford, p 59 NCH, p 158 / Payton, p 37.

37. Manders, p 49.

38. Manders, p 49. The de Birmingham's were henceforth the hereditary stewards of the Barons of Dudley.

39. Misc. In. R.of D, Vol. I, p 67.

40. Ratcliffe, p 243.

41. Carter, p 25.

42. Dugdale, Baronage, Vol. I, p 612.

43. Dugdale. Vol. I, p 612. / Grazebrook, p 9.

44. Grazebrook, p 11. / Liber. Niger, Pipe Rolls, 9 Rich I.

45. Grazebrook, p 13.

46. Rollason, p 1.

47. Carter, p 28.

48. Pipe Rolls: Bucks, I, p 150. / Pipe Rolls: Berks, II, and p 156.

49. Evidence for this was that Salisbury was assessed for the Dudley scutage of 50 knight's fees but did not pay it because he attended the king in France, Grazebrook, p 14.

50. Grazebrook, p 15.

51. Carter, p 29.

52. Carter, p 28. Many of the lands never did come back to the Barony of Dudley!

53. Rot. Lit. Claus. 1216, Ranulf was said to hold the Barony of Dudley. This means Ralph II was dead and William was considered to be the next lord when he reached maturity. Kings made a small fortune out of wardships. They were sold to great lords who would draw of their wards estates to pay for their expenses, needless to say this was often open to exploitation. VCH, p 91.

54. Grazebrook, p 14.

55. Nash, Vol. II, p 207/Grazebrook, p 15.

56. Carter, p 30.

57. Fine Rolls, R of D, Vol. I, p 185. /Grazebrook, p 16. This rather destroys

Carter's argument that there is no evidence that Nicholas was in line for the barony.

58. Charter Rolls, R.of D.,Vol. II, p 60.
59. VCH, I, p 91. / Grazebrook, p 15. A Writ of Protection was a document signed by the king that while away on foreign service he would guarantee the safety of that person's property for the duration of his service.
60. Barrow, p 260/ Carter p 31.
61. Grazebrook, p 17. /Blocksidge, p 32.
62. Dugdale/ Grazebrook. p 16/ Carter, p 31. The only evidence for Roger's death is a statement by Dugdale. There is no reference in the Close Rolls, (which there should have been), so Grazebrook concludes that Roger did not die till 1278. He is forgetting of course Roger's estates had been taken into the king's hands in 1232 and there is no evidence of him getting them back, so there is no reason why he should be referred to in the rolls of 1235. I believe Dugdale and Carter are correct so Grazebrook's Roger I part two, is my Roger II.
63. Chandler & Hannah, p 19. Nicola was sister to William D'Albini, Earl of Arundel and Hugh D'Albini, Earl of Surrey, very powerful men!
64. VCH, p 98.
65. Salt, Plea Rolls, Wrottesley Vol IV.
66. Carter, p 34.
67. Chandler& Hannah, p 19. Roger was Amabel's second husband, her first died in 1254.
68. Grazebrook, p 19. The letters of Protection was dated 20th May 1253. Roger's right of free warren and Clent Fair was signed in Gascony.
69. Grazebrook p 19.
70. Grazebrook, p 19.
71. Blanow, p 130. Close Rolls
72. Patent Rolls, Rof D Vol. II, p 22. /Grazebrook, p 19.
73. Hutton.
74. VCH (Staffs), p 228. Interestingly William de Birmingham fought on the baron's side against his feudal lord. Blanow, p 129-30. John Fitzalan's mother was Isabella D'Albini sister to Roger I's first wife.
75. On de Montfort's side was also Roger's son-in-law Ralph de Bassett who refused to leave him. It was probably his relationship with Roger's daughter Margaret that saved him from loosing all his lands. Blanow, p 162. As part of Margaret's dowery Roger gave Ralph Olney in Buckinghamshire. Close Rolls, Ed 11288-96. Their son Roger was given part of the manor of Walsall by John de Somery in1317. John had acquired it in 1311 from Roger de Morteyn.

76. Grazebrook, p 20.

77. IPM, Close Rolls; his wife Amabel was also given the dowery lands of Dudley on his death (Bradfield, Swinford, Clent, Bordesley, Cradley and Sedgley Park) as well as other lands by the king in gratitude for the services of her late husband.

78. Final Concord, R of D, Vol. 2.

79. Close Rolls, R of D, Vol. 2, and p 3.

80. Close Rolls, R of D, Vol. 2, and p 3.

81. Fine Rolls, R of D, Vol.2.

82. Salt, Close Rolls Vol VI p 100.

83. Wrottesley, (1887) Services performed by the Staffordshire tenants in the 13th and 14th century, Stafford.

84. J Chancellor/ Charles Knightly/ A Bryant.

85. Grazebrook, P .30, Forest Court Presentments (1286)

86. Radford, p 453/ Payton, p 40.

87. Patent Roll, Rof D, Vol. II, p 22.

88. Patent Rolls, Rof D, Vol. II, p 23.

89. Dugdale stated John fought in both campaigns. Grazebrook could not find him in the earlier one in the Scottish Roll of Staffordshire tenants, (p.4 1), but there are other rolls which Dugdale may have used. Misc. Inquis. R.of D.,Vol. II, p 62.

90. Misc. Inquis. Rof D, Vol. II, p 63.

91. Carter, p 39/ Grazebrook, p 41.

92. Plea Rolls. Grazebrook, p 40. Carter suggests it was before the July.

93. Grazebrook, p 41.

94. Carter, p 39.

95. VCH, p 91. (Abbrev. Rot. Orig.) He did homage for his lands on 31st March 1310. Fine Rolls.

96. Rollason, p 2.

97. Grazebrook, p 41.

98. Grazebrook, p 41. / Close Rolls Rof D, Vol. II, and p 24.

99. Fine rolls, Wrottesley 1307-1327, C of H of ST IX.

100. Patent Rolls

10l. Pat Rolls

102. Gross, p 34. There was a close relationship between these men: Roger Mortimer's daughter married Charlton's son whose sister was married to John de Sutton.

103. Grazebrook, p 42. / Patent Rolls pl. i. m. 12d. / Cal. Patent 1307-1313 p 369. VCH p 91.

104. Gross, p 34-39. John received a licence from the king to give Ralph Bassett part of his holding of the Manor of Walsall./Grazebrook, p 41.
105. VCH, p 92.
106. Fine Rolls, Wrottesley 1307-1327 C of H ST IX.
107. Underhill, p 46.
108. Grazebrook, p 42.
109. 1323 Thomas de Cobham's Register/Pearce, 1930, p 148.
110. Grazebrook, p 46.
111. Close Rolls
112. Grazebrook, p 51.
113. Wrottesley De Banco Rolls: Ralph Bassett sued the Sutton's and the Botetourt's in 1323 regarding Lucy de Somery's claim to the moiety of the Manor of Walsall and the following year Sara Fitzphilip sued them for a third part of Bobbington also part of Lucy's dower.
114. Bingham, p 145.
115. Close Rolls, Rof D, Vol. II, p 8. / Misc. Inquis. R of D, Vol. II, p 65.
116. Close Rolls, Rof D, Vol. II, p 6.
117. Close Rolls, Rof D, Vol. II, p 10.
118. Grazebrook, p 52.
119. According to the Assize Rolls Joan also claimed half of the Castle. V.C.H. p 92. She had no right to it as Letters Patent dated May 1340 stated categorically that the castle was settled on John's wife Isabella.
120. Patent Rolls, Rof D, Vol. II, p 28.
121. Printed Calendar Patent Rolls, 12.Ed.III, m.21, p 133. /Grazebrook, p 53.
122. VCH, p 92. John, it appears, did not have any letters patent confirming his right to the castle and town at Dudley until this time. The castle itself was settled in the hands of Isabella, his wife.
123. Grazebrook. p 56. The writ was issued to John personally; the lords of Dudley never had the right of automatically being called to Parliament.
124. Bryant, p 287-289.
125. In the Middle Ages the year started on Lady Day (March 25th) so their January 1343 was our 1344!
126. Wrottesley Crecy to Calais, Salt, Vol. xviii.
127. Razi. Z, Life, Death and Marriage in a Medieval Parish, Cambridge.
128. Patent Rolls, R of D, Vol. II, p 15.
129. Patent Rolls, R of D, Vol. II, p 36.
130. Grazebrook, p 53.
131. Grazebrook p 55. / Close Rolls, R.of D., Vol. II, p 14.

132. Claude Dudley felt that Richard Dudley was a Clapton due to the similarity in their coat-of-arms. p 11.

133. Blocksidge.

134. Salt, License.

135. Colvin,

136. Patent Rolls, Rof D, Vol. II, p 38.

137. VCH, p 161.

138. Salt, Ple. Rol./Grazebrook, p 59.

139. Grazebrook, p 60.

140. Salt.

141. Rollason.

142. Grazebrook, p 62 /Close Rolls, R.of D., Vol. II, p 17.

143. Rof D, Vol. III, p 65/ Brit. Mus: Oct Charter X4.

144. Macdonald, p 65.

145. Grazebrook, p 63.

146. Guttery, p 10.

147. Guttery, p 8, 26/Fine Rolls, Rof D, Vol. II, p 58.

148. Grazebrook p 65.

149. Grazebrook. p 65.

150. Patent Rolls, Rof D, Vol. II, p 44, p 204.

151. Patent Rolls 1422-29, p 204.

152. Patent Rolls 1422-29, p 475, 493.

153. Nicholson, p 218-7

154. Guttery p 27.

155. Guttery p 39

156. Guttery, p 42.

157. Underhill, p 62.

158. Storey, p 67.

159. Myers, Rot. Parl. v 216b, p 207, 154.

160. Storey, p 135.

161. Falkus,p .35.

162. Myers, p 154.

163. Kendall, P. 28-29.

164. Warrington, Bk. I, p 102.

165. Grazebrook, p 67.

166. Kendle, p 52-53.

167. Green, p 279.

169. Mag. Reg., Salt Collection.

169. Close Rolls, Salt Collection.

170. Close Rolls, Salt Collection.

171. VCH, p 92.

172. Rollason.

173. Tilley, p 3.

174. R. Tilley, p 4.

175. Grazebrook, p 69.

176. Patent Rolls, Rof D, Vol. II, p45.

177. Rolls.

178. I.P.M. PRO.

179. Grazebrook, p 79.

180. Mem. Rol.

181. VCH, L&PH VIII V.1727.

182. Chancery. P.R.O.

183. Pat. Rolls, PRO / Cor. of Exch. E315/291.

184. L&p Hviii XIII(2) App 6.

185. Beer, p 6.

186. Beer, Northumberland,/Mary Rose Trust. The Mary Rose has recently been raised and is now an exhibit in the Royal Dock Yard at Portsmouth.

187. Public Record Office, Mins. & Rec. Acc. / R.of D., Vol. II, p 17.

188. Chancery Proceedings, Rof D Vol. II, P. 75 / Memoranda, Rof D, Vol. I, p 64.

189. Holinshead, p 98.

190. Grazebrook, p 75.

191. Cotton MS Nero C.X. f.51. English Historical Documents p 40.

192. V.C.H.

193. Beer, p 61.

194. Patent Rolls, Rof D, Vol. II, p 49.

195. Patent Rolls, Rof D, Vol. II, p 50. /Grazebrook, p 105.

196. Nichols, p 299.

197. Grazebrook, p 104-107.

198. Fraser, p 26.

199. State Papers: Domestic.

200. Sergeant, WHS, 1952-1957.

201. Nichols p 544.

202. Grazebrook, p l04.

203. Grazebrook, p 107.

204. Court of Exchequer, Rof D Vol. I, p 4 - p17. / Memoranda Rolls Rof D Vol. I, p 62.

205. R of D, Vol. 1, p.4.

206. Court of Exchequer, Rof D Vol. I, p 9 - p 15.
207. Grazebrook, p 109-111./Court of Exchequer, Rof D Vol. I, p 11.
208. King, P.
209. Grazebrook p 118.
210. Willis Bund.
211. Facsimile of contemporary broadsheet.
212. V.C.H./Hollies.
213. p 142-3.
214. Sherwood, 1974, p 106, 112-115.
215. Johnson & Gainey, P.44. (S.R.O., D.260/M/PV/1)
216. Coll. His Staff 1941, p 138-139.
217. Sherwood,1974, p 95.
218. Sherwood, 1974, p 94-5.
219. Sherwood, 1974, p I.13.
220. Sherwood,1974, p 14.
221. Sherwood,1974, p 14.
222. Domestic Papers-Charles I, p 235-236.
223. Sherwood, 1974, p 114
224. p 141
225. Travellers Guide to the Battlefields of the English Civil War, Martyn Bennett, 1990, p 112.
226. Noake, 1856, p 239.
227. Sherwood, 1974, p 167.
228. Travellers Guide to the Battlefields of the English Civil War, Martyn Bennett, 1990, p 158.]
229. Hist. of Staff, 1941, p 145.
230. Hemingway, Brereton Letter book
231. Sherwood, 1974, p 11
232. Johnson & Oiney p 69. S.O., D.260/M/F/1/6, f8.
233. Coll. Hist. of Staffs, 1941, p 145.
234. Grazebrook, p 113 / 209. Hemingway, p 97.
235. Grazebrook, p 120-121.
236. Grazebrook, p 121.
237. Estate Papers at Archive, Coseley.
238. Grazebrook, p 120.
239. Grazebrook, p 121.
240. Blocksidge, p 21.
241. Raybould, p 31.
242. Grazebrook, p 121.

243. Grazebrook, p 122.
244. Grazebrook, p 129. William and Ferdinando were second cousins.
245. Monro Purkis, p 31.
246. Williams, 1939, p 135.
247. Steve Linnane, p 19-24 (1997).
248. Steve Linnane, p 16-21 (2004).
249. A copy of this Inventory was given by the William Salt Library, Stafford to the DUCAP project on 18th February 1982.
250. Steve Linnane, p 28-31 (1993).
251. Steve Linnane, p 6-9 (1993).
252. Joan Tyson, p 9 (1999).
253. Steve Linnane, p 29-30 (1993).

Appendix 1 - Time-line

1066 Battle of Hastings

1070 Earl Edwin Assassinated

1070 Building of Motte and Bailey at Dudley

1135-1153 The Anarchy (Civil War)

1138 Siege of Dudley Castle

1153 Duke Henry Plantagenet, later King Henry II at Dudley Castle.

1173 Baron's Rebellion

1173 Dudley Castle Sleighted

1175 Gervase Paganell left Dudley

1229 Roger De Somery I came back to Dudley Castle

1262 Roger II began to re fortify Dudley Castle, King stopped him

1263 King gave Roger a licence to re-fortify Dudley Castle

1265 Simon de Montfort's Parliament

1272 Castle newly commenced when Roger died

1276-1282 Anglo-Welsh War

1295-1307 Anglo-Scottish War, part one.

1322 John De Somery died, Great Chamber complex was complete as chapel was recorded as being in use

1325 John de Sutton arrested for implication in the Lancaster Rebellion. He was forced into handing over his castle and lands to the Despencers.

1326 John de Sutton was given his Castle and lands back

1327 King Edward III, Queen Isabella and Roger Mortimer guests at Dudley Castle

1333 Anglo-Scottish War, part two.

1337 Start of Hundred Years War against
the French
1346 Battle of Crecy
1349 Black Death came to England
1356 Battle of Poitier

[The Sutton's fought in most of the battles in the 14th and 15th centuries]

1381 Peasants Revolt
1415 Battle of Agincourt
1428 Joan of Arc led French attack
1453 Hundred Years War came to an end
1454 Wars of the Roses begins
1485 Battle of Bosworth, End of the War
of the Roses

1470's Barbican and Kitchen Annex built

1534 Henry VIII declared him self
to be head of the Church in England.

1537 John Dudley bought up John Sutton's mortgages.
1540's John Dudley had the Sharrington Range built.
1575 Queen Elizabeth Ist stayed at Dudley Castle.

1589 Spanish Armada
1641-1651 Civil War

Castle held for the king.
1643 First Siege of Dudley Castle
1646 Second Siege of Dudley Castle
1647 The defences of the castle were sleighted by order of Parliament
1652 The castle was sequestered
1656 The castle was returned to the Wards

1685 Monmouth Rebellion
1715 First Jacobite Rebellion
1745 Second Jacobite Rebellion

1750 The domestic quarters caught fire and castle left a ruin

Appendix 2 - A selection of images of the Castle.

Above: Motte and Bailey at Dudley, c1086. Paul Whitehouse, Source: DUCAP
Below: Dudley Castle c 1764. George Molineux, Source: Dudley Art Gallery

D U D L E Y   C A S T L E,   S T A F F O R D S H I R E.

Above: Internal Dudley Castle, looking north. 1785, DL, Source Dudley Art Gallery

Below: Gateway at Dudley Castle. Phillip James de Loutherbourg, c 1805, Source: Dudley Art Gallery

DUDLEY CASTLE.
Principal Entrance & Keep

F. Bissell del! lith.

Above & below - Source: Birmingham Reference Library, 19th Century

DUDLEY CASTLE
From the Keep
Printed at T Underwoods Lithographic Establishment
Cherry St Birmingham

172

Index

Emold, Nicholas 44
Empress Matilda 22
Enville 15
Evesham 36

F
Ffradshaw, Captain 99

G
Gascony 40, 56, 59, 66
Gaveston, Piers 43
Gloucester 38, 64, 66, 67
Glyndwr, Owain 63
Gower 52
Great Chamber 39, 129
Great Charter 36
Grey, Lady Jane 73, 82
Grosvenor, Martha 90
Guilford, Jane 76

H
Halesowen 58, 60, 84, 119
Hamble 22
Harrington, Theodosia 86
Heaveningham, Christopher 94, 105, 109
Henry I 22
Henry II 26
Henry III 33, 34
Henry Plantagenet 23, 24
Henry V 64
Henry VI 66
Henry VII 70, 76
Henry VIII 71, 77
Hereford 13, 35, 36, 53
Hereward the Wake 13
Himley 15, 50, 57, 60, 63, 65, 69, 74, 75, 83, 86, 110
Howard of Effingham 89

I
Inkpen 24, 27

J
John of Gaunt 63

K
Kates Hill 95
Kenilworth 45, 54

N

O

P

Q

R

S